This book is most lovingly dedicated to:

Jennifer and Jessica—may they always love
reading

Authors, editors, and publishers—for the
good they do

And most important, Beverly—my most favorite
January author

ABOUT THE AUTHOR

David Fiday earned his B.A. and M.A. degrees in Instructional Technology from Northern Illinois University in DeKalb. He has done graduate work with computers and has taught computer seminars and classes for a local junior college and university. Mr. Fiday has been a media specialist since 1975, during which time he worked in the Bolingbrook and Laraway school districts in Illinois. He is currently the media director for the Palos East Elementary School in Palos Heights, Illinois.

He has published articles and stories in various teacher, computer, and children's magazines, and has coauthored *Time to Go* (Harcourt Brace Jovanovich, 1990) with Beverly Fiday. His other published stories include *Ears, Eyes, Nose, and Mouth* and *Sweet Surprises*, both from Standard Publishing.

Mr. Fiday enjoys teaching children and teachers about good authors through his daily teaching assignments and special workshops in local school districts. He believes that reading, writing, art, and author studies are a natural subject for media centers and libraries. "We should relish them and the relationship they share." His main ambition is to continue writing children's books and resource materials for teachers. "Teachers need to know what good books are available and the appropriate grade level. They are often too busy for a class, so this book is an effort to help them begin the search for good books for their students."

AUTHORS AND ILLUSTRATORS THROUGH THE YEAR

Ready-to-Use Literature Activities for Grades K–3

David J. Fiday

THE CENTER FOR APPLIED
RESEARCH IN EDUCATION
West Nyack, New York 10995

10 9 8 7 6 5 4

GRAPHICS BY "THE PRINT SHOP" BRODERBUND SOFTWARE INC., 1984.
Crossword puzzles created with "Crossword Magic" by Mindscape, 1981.
Wordsearch puzzles created with "Puzzles and Posters" by MECC, 1983.

Library of Congress Cataloging-in-Publication Data

Fiday, David.
    Authors and illustrators through the year : ready-to-use
literature activities for grades K-3/David J. Fiday.
        p.   cm.
    Includes bibliographies.
    ISBN 0-87628-001-7
    1. School libraries—Activity programs.   2. Libraries, Children's-
-Activity programs.   3. Children's literature—Study and teaching
(Primary)   4. Children—Books and reading.   I. Title.
Z675.S3F45   1989
027.8'222—dc20   89-9978
                                                                                        CIP

ISBN 0-87628-001-7

**THE CENTER FOR APPLIED
RESEARCH IN EDUCATION**
BUSINESS & PROFESSIONAL DIVISION
A division of Simon & Schuster
West Nyack, New York 10995

Printed in the United States of America

About This Book

Authors and Illustrators Through the Year brings children and good books together. It offers classroom teachers and library media specialists the opportunity to let children read good books, find authors at or near their reading level, and develop a most important life-long attitude—reading for pleasure.

Students can easily read, write, and draw their way through the year using the more than 150 book titles and accompanying ready-to-use, reproducible activity sheets.

Contents

Authors and Illustrators Through the Year can be arranged as a series of calendars big enough for all students to see and read. (See "How to Make the Calendar" later in this section.)

Each month includes:

- A monthly table of contents listing the authors and/or illustrators, their book, and activities to extend students' reading/listening experiences.
- An author sheet listing the authors of that month with their birthdates, if the person is an author and/or illustrator, and the reading level.
- Activity sheets that can be reproduced as many times as needed, including reading activities (fill-in-the-blanks, word searches, crossword puzzles, story sequence), writing activities (group story projects, individual stories, short-answer, poem-writing, personal information), and drawing activities.
- Bookmarks to encourage reading and to celebrate seasons and holidays.
- A complete answer key to that month's activity sheets.
- Bibliographies of that month's authors.

How to Use

After you have created the calendar, introduce your students to its use. Here are a few ways to start:

1. Students may view the calendar and select an author's book to find. They read the book and complete the activity sheet.
2. Specific titles might be read to the children.

3. Library media specialists may suggest specific titles and activity sheets for classroom use by teachers.
4. When a short period of time exists in the daily schedule, a great story and followup activity are the perfect solution.
5. Children may select an author of a series and start reading all of his or her books.
6. If some children share a birthday with an author, they may want to read "their author" first.
7. Each child reads his or her birthday author (or one near his or her birthday), gives a book report, and has a classmate read the book. This sharing and swapping encourages and motivates reading.

For the Classroom Teacher

Teachers in self-contained elementary classrooms may want to create a reading support program with the materials contained in this book. Here are additional ways to incorporate these books into your existing program:

1. Tell the children that you are going to give them their own "Authors' Reading Corner." Create the calendar, make a display, and designate an area (reading table, a corner, or a carpeted area) in which the children read their books and do their activity sheets.
2. Display selected titles from the month and place copies of the activity sheets in nearby folders. Label each folder with the title of the book.
3. Read one book to the children and complete the activity sheet with them.
4. Explain to the children that they may read any title and complete the activity sheet when you are working with another reading group.
5. Change the collection each month.

For the Library Media Specialist

This book is a large resource. As such, the manner of organization can be either on a large scale or a simple operation, depending on your particular needs. Copies of the activity sheets can be kept in file folders. When a student selects a specific author, the activity sheet can be given to the student at the same time. Abler students may select their own activity sheets after they have read the book.

A Final Word

You might notice that certain well-known and well-loved authors (such as John Barrett, Dorothy Haas, and Shel Silverstein) are not included. Research and investigation are continuing so that missing notables can be included in a possible future edition of this book.

In the meantime, this edition of *Authors and Illustrators Through the Year* is a compendium, a gift from many people who love children and storytelling. I hope that I will have a small part in helping the love of reading grow from one generation to another with your help. Enjoy!

David J. Fiday

How to Make the Calendar

Calendar Idea One

1. Use two oversized calendars available from a teacher supply store or make them from posterboard. Hang two calendars each month to offer children a variety of authors. Start the school year with August and September, and include July at the end of the school year in June.

2. Cut blank card catalog cards or unlined 3″ × 5″ index cards to 2″ × 2″ squares that fit within each daily space.

3. Use a hole-punch to make a hole in the appropriate spot as shown in the illustration.

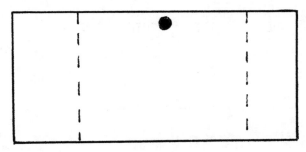

4. Write the date and the author's name as shown in the illustration.

5. Stick pins into the date squares and hang the appropriate authors' birthdates in sequence. This movable card format allows you to easily change the authors each month.

6. You might want to add a "Happy Birthday" banner (either store-bought or teacher-made) to increase the atmosphere of celebration. A "Happy Birthday Authors and Illustrators" banner can also be made with certain computer software programs, such as "Print Shop," available from Broderbund Software, 17 Paul Drive, San Rafael, CA 94903.

Calendar Idea Two

You might want to focus on a "(month)'s Featured Authors" display. The computer program called "Print Shop Companion" can be used to make a calendar similar to the one shown here.

SUN	MON	TUE	WED	THU	FRI	SAT
					1 MAKE A SEPTEMBER BOOKMARK	**2** BERNARD MOST
3 ALIKI BRANDENBURG (ALIKI)	**4** SYD HOFF	**5** READ A MAGAZINE	**6** FELIX SALTEN	**7** ELMER HADER	**8** BYRON BARTON / MICHAEL HAGUE / JACK PRELUTSKY	**9** AILEEN FISHER
10 READ PART OF YOUR BOOK TO MOM OR DAD	**11** ALFRED SLOTE	**12** LISTEN TO ONE OF YOUR FRIENDS READ.	**13** ELSE HOLMELUND MINARIK / ROALD DAHL	**'14** EDITH THACHER HURD / ROBYN SUPRANER / DIANE GOODE / JOHN STEPTOE	**15** WATTE PIPER / TOMIE DE PAOLA / ROBERT MCCLOSKEY	**16** JANET SCHULMAN / H.A. REY
17 PAUL GOBLE	**18** READ DURING RECESS-- IF IT'S TOO HOT TO RUN. FIND A NICE COOL TREE.	**19** RACHEL FIELD	**20** GET A JUMP ON EVERYBODY-- READ CROW BOY TODAY!	**21** TARO YASHIMA	**22** READ ANOTHER TITLE BY RORLD DAHL	**23** JOAN FASSLER
24 IAN SERRAILLER	**25** READ ANOTHER TITLE BY BERNARD MOST	**26** READ A MAGAZINE. TRY SCIENCELAND.	**27** BERNARD WABER / DONALD ARTHUR TORGERSEN	**28** READ A CALDECOTT AWARD BOOK!	**29** STAN BERENSTAIN	**30** EDGAR D'AULAIRE / ALVIN TRESSELT

WELCOME BACK READERS

Copies of this calendar can be given to children for individual use. Print the filled-in calendar on one side of the paper, and a blank calendar on the other side. The students can then color in with crayon the squares of the authors they read. If they choose, students can use the blank calendar as follows:

- Write the last name of the author read in today's date.
- Color the square.
- If more than one author is read in a day, write all their last names in the date square and color it.
- Books from home, those from friends, or those given as gifts could also be included on the calendar.

Contents

OCTOBER • 27

NOVEMBER • 51

DECEMBER • 75

JANUARY • 101

Kay Chorao, *Lester's Overnight*
Remy Charlip, *Fortunately*
Raymond Briggs, *The Snowman*
A. A. Milne, "Write a Poem"
Arthur Ransome, *The Fool of the World and the Flying Ship*
Blair Lent, *The Funny Little Woman*
Harry Allard, *Miss Nelson Is Missing*
Bill Peet, *Big Bad Bruce*
Rosemary Wells, *Noisy Nora*
Gerald McDermott, *Arrow to the Sun*

FEBRUARY • 129

Activity Sheets:

Joan Lowrey Nixon, *The Valentine Mystery*
Russell Hoban, *Bread and Jam for Frances*
Adrienne Adams, *The Shoemaker and the Elves*
Dick Gackenbach, *Harry and the Terrible Whatzit*
Jane Yolen, *Owl Moon*
Judy Blume, *The One in the Middle Is a Green Kangaroo*
"Send a Valentine to Your Favorite Author"
Mike Thaler, *There's a Hippopotamus Under My Bed*
Norman Bridwell, *Witch Next Door*
David & Beverly Fiday, *Time to Go*
David Fiday, "Send Me a Note"
Wilhelm Grimm, *Snow White*
Florence Parry Heide, *The Shrinking of Treehorn*
Uri Shulevitz, *The Treasure*

MARCH • 153

APRIL • 175

Chris Van Allsburg, *The Polar Express*
Chris Van Allsburg, *Mysteries of Harris Burdick*
Robert Kraus, *How Spider Saved Halloween*
Eric Carle, *Very Hungry Caterpillar*
Nancy Willard, *Papa's Panda*
Charlotte Zolotow, *Someday*
David McPhail, *Emma's Vacation*

JULY • 251

Activity Sheets:

Jack Gantos, *Rotten Ralph*
Martin Provensen, *Year at Maple Hill Farm*
Marcia Brown, *Once a Mouse*
Peggy Parish, *Play Ball, Amelia Bedelia*
Walter Edmonds, *The Matchlock Gun*
Clement C. Moore, *The Night Before Christmas*
Richard Egielski, *Mary's Mirror*
Eve Merriam, *Good Night to Annie*
Margery Williams, *The Velveteen Rabbit*
Patricia Coombs, *Dorrie and the Blue Witch*
Robert Quackenbush, *Dig to Disaster*
Jan Berenstain, *The Berenstain Bears Go to Camp*
Beatrix Potter, *The Tale of Peter Rabbit*

AUGUST • 273

Activity Sheets:

James Howe, *There's a Monster Under My Bed*
Frank Asch, *Moongame* and *Mooncake*

Trinka Hakes Noble, *The Day Jimmy's Boa Ate the Wash*

Don Freeman, *A Rainbow of My Own*

Steven Kroll, *The Tyrannosaurus Game*

Robert Crowe, *Clyde Monster*

Alice Provensen, *The Glorious Flight Across the Channel with Louis Bieriot*

Brinton Turkle, *Thy Friend, Obadiah*

Arthur Yorinks, *Hey, Al* and *It Happened in Pinsk*

Roger Duvoisin, *Petunia, I Love You*

Virginia Lee Burton, *The Little House*

SEPTEMBER

September 2	Bernard Most, *If the Dinosaurs Came Back* (writing activity)
September 4	Syd Hoff, *Chester, Julius, Grizzwold* (short answers)
September 7	Elmer Hader, *The Big Snow* (fill in)
September 8	Jack Prelutsky, *The New Kid on the Block* (writing poems)
September 13	Roald Dahl, *Roald Dahl's Revolting Rhymes* (short-answer comparison)
September 13	Else Holmelund Minarik, *Little Bear's Visit* (alphabetical order)
September 14	Edith Thacher Hurd, *Johnny Lion's Bad Day* (definitions)
September 14	Diane Goode, *When I Was Young in the Mountains* (short-answer biography writing activity)
September 15	Tomie DePaola, *Strega Nona* (a Strega Nona cookbook)
September 16	H.A. Rey, *Curious George Visits the Zoo* (fill in)
September 17	Paul Goble, *Buffalo Woman* (crossword puzzle)
September 21	Taro Yashima, *Crow Boy* (short-answer special test)
September 27	Don Torgersen, *Huff and Puff and the Troll Hole* (fill in)
September 27	Bernard Waber, *Ira Sleeps Over* (sequence story events/writing sheet)
September 29	Stan Berenstain, *The Berenstain Bears No Girls Allowed* (feelings chart)
September 30	Alvin Tresselt, *The Mitten* (alphabetical order)

September Bookmarks
September Answer Key
September Authors Bibliography

 # SEPTEMBER AUTHORS

DATE	NAME	AUTHOR	ILLUSTRATOR	READING LEVEL			
				K	1	2	3
2	Bernard Most	X	X	X	X	X	
3	Aliki Brandenberg	X	X		X	X	X
4	Syd Hoff	X	X	X	X	X	
6	Felix Salten	X					X
7	Elmer Hader	X	X			X	X
8	Byron Barton	X	X			X	X
8	Michael Hague		X				
8	Jack Prelutsky	X		X	X	X	X
9	Aileen Fisher	X				X	
11	Alfred Slote	X					X
13	Else Holmelund Minarik	X		X	X	X	
13	Roald Dahl	X					X
14	Edith Thacher Hurd	X			X	X	
14	John Steptoe	X				X	X
14	Diane Goode		X				
14	Robyn Supraner	X				X	X
15	Watty Piper	X			X	X	
15	Tomie DePaola	X	X		X	X	
15	Robert McCloskey	X	X		X	X	X
16	Janet Schulman	X					X
16	H.A. Rey	X	X	X	X	X	
17	Paul Goble	X	X			X	X
19	Rachel Field	X			X	X	
21	Taro Yashima	X	X		X	X	
23	Joan Fassler	X				X	X
24	Ian Serrailler	X				X	X
27	Bernard Waber	X	X	X	X	X	
27	Donald Torgersen	X				X	X
29	Stan Berenstain	X	X	X	X	X	
30	Edgar D'aulaire	X	X			X	X
30	Alvin Tresselt	X				X	X

BERNARD MOST

"If The Dinosaurs Came Back"

Draw your pet dinosaur in the space below. Write 3 sentences or more that tell what you and your dinosaur like to do best. If everyone in your room does this activity, you will have a class dinosaur book!

Name_____ **Date**_____

SYD HOFF

"Chester; Julius; Grizzwold"

Read "Chester," "Julius," or "Grizzwold." Answer the questions below.

1. What was the problem in the story?

_____

_____

_____

2. What did he like to do?

_____

_____

_____

3. How did he help people?

_____

_____

_____

4. How did he solve his problem?

_____

_____

_____

Name_____ Date_____

ELMER HADER

"The Big Snow"

Read "The Big Snow." Use the words in the Word Bank to answer the questions below.

1. For a warm coat of fur, eat lots of _____ leaves and carrot _____.

2. A groundhog sleeps until _____.

3. Chipmunks store seeds and _____.

4. Bluejays fly _____.

5. Cardinals stay. They like _____.

6. _____ and _____ squirrels store nuts and acorns.

7. Raccoons stay warm in _____ trunks.

8. A _____ of snow covered everything.

WORD BANK

blanket	grey	nuts	south	tops
cabbage	hollow	red	spring	winter

Name _____   **Date** _____

JACK PRELUTSKY

"The New Kid on the Block"

_____

Read "Underwater Wibbles," "Snillies," and "The Bloders Are Exploding" in "The New Kid on the Block." Write a poem about a new kind of creature that you create. Use these questions as a guide to help you think.

1. What is the name of your creature? Examples: Gibbles, Gubbles, Jillies, Kissies, or Gobbles.

2. What does your creature like to do best? Examples: Gibbles are always talking gibberish, Kissies are always kissing (like moms and dads), Gobbles are always hungry, especially after reading a good book.

3. Where does your creature live? Example: Gobbles live in cupboards so they don't need to walk too far for their next meal. You can blame them when you find a cereal box with an open seal.

4. Do your best to make it rhyme. To think of the right words, give yourself plenty of time.

5. Practice your creature poem on the lines below. When you have a perfect poem, write it neatly on a clean piece of paper. If you feel creative, draw a picture of your creature.

_____
Title

_____

_____

_____

_____

_____

_____

_____

Name _____ **Date** _____

© 1989 by The Center for Applied Research in Education

ROALD DAHL

"Roald Dahl's Revolting Rhymes"

_____

Read "The Three Little Pigs" story from "Roald Dahl's Revolting Rhymes."

1. List three ideas that are the same as in the original story.

_____

_____

_____

2. List as many ideas as you can that are different.

_____

_____

_____

3. Read another story from Dahl's "Revolting Rhymes."

Write the title here: _____

4. Write the ideas that are the:

SAME   DIFFERENT

_____   _____

_____   _____

_____   _____

_____   _____

Now that you know what a great author Roald is, why don't you try to rewrite a fairy tale of your own. It doesn't need to rhyme. Try your best on a clean piece of paper.

Name_____   Date_____

ELSE HOLMELUND MINARIK

"Little Bear's Visit"

Put the words from the Word Bank into alphabetical order.

1. _____
2. _____
3. _____
4. _____
5. _____
6. _____
7. _____
8. _____
9. _____
10. _____
11. _____
12. _____

13. _____
14. _____
15. _____
16. _____
17. _____
18. _____
19. _____
20. _____
21. _____
22. _____
23. _____
24. _____

WORD BANK					
hat	visit	jig	garden	toy	woods
paws	skip	bread	jam	bear	summer
robin	spring	nest	window	sky	fly
sang	sad	kiss	come	back	free

Name _____   Date _____

EDITH THACHER HURD

"Johnny Lion's Bad Day"

Read "Johnny Lion's Bad Day." Match the words from the Word Bank to their definitions.

1. ___ ___ ___   not good

2. ___ ___ ___   place to sleep

3. ___ ___ ___   before night

4. ___ ___ ___   king of night bird

5. ___ ___ ___ ___   see with these

6. ___ ___ ___   large

7. ___ ___ ___ ___ ___ ___   hops a lot

8. ___ ___ ___ ___   make food ready

9. ___ ___ ___   cook in this

10. ___ ___ ___ ___ ___ ___ ___   sneeze

> **WORD BANK**
>
> | bad | cook | kerchew | rabbit |
> |-----|------|---------|--------|
> | bed | day | owl | |
> | big | eyes | pot | |

Johnny Lion had a bad day. He couldn't get out of bed. He had bad dreams from his medicine. Use the back of this sheet to write about the last bad dream you had. If you don't have bad dreams, make one up!

Name_____   Date_____

 # DIANE GOODE

"When I Was Young in the Mountains"

Read "When I Was Young in the Mountains". Answer these questions to tell what you remember best about being young.

1. When I was young in _____.

2. Grandpa worked a _____.

3. Grandma made the best _____.

4. I'll never forget when Dad _____.

5. Mom always _____.

6. One Christmas, Santa brought me a _____.

Write three more sentences about the thing you will always remember.

_____

_____

_____

_____

_____

Name_____ Date_____

 # TOMIE DEPAOLA

"Our Strega Nona Cook Book"

Write the following information in the cooking pot. Share your favorite recipe with your classmates.

1. What is the name of your favorite food?
2. What ingredients do you need? How much of each?
3. How should they be combined?
4. At what temperature should they be baked? (if it applies)
5. How long should it be baked or cooked?
6. Are there any special serving instructions?

If everyone in your classroom does this activity, you will have a Classroom Cook Book.

Name_____ Date_____

H. A. REY

"Curious George Visits the Zoo"

Read "Curious George Visits the Zoo." Use the Words in the Word Bank to finish the sentences.

1. Curious George went to the _____.

2. He saw giraffes with long _____.

3. Kangaroos have _____.

4. Elephants have floppy _____ and long _____.

5. Zookeepers feed the _____.

6. Monkeys like to eat _____.

7. Curious George grabbed a _____.

8. A little boy lost his red _____.

9. Curious George _____ the bananas to the monkeys.

10. Curious George gave the balloon back to the little _____.

WORD BANK				
animals	balloon	bananas	boy	bucket
ears	fed	necks	pockets	trunks
zoo				

Name_____   Date_____

PAUL GOBLE

"Buffalo Woman"

Read "Buffalo Woman." Use the words in the Word Bank to answer the crossword puzzle.

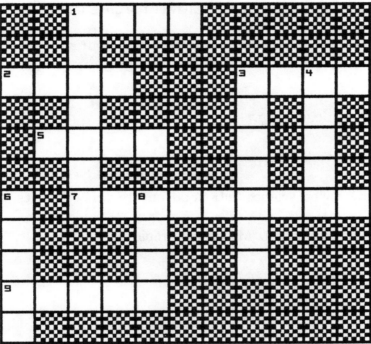

ACROSS CLUES
1. FLESH OF ANIMAL
2. GROUP
3. STICKER
5. HIDE HOUSE
7. PAINTED
9. LEADER

DOWN CLUES
1. HUSBAND AND WIFE
3. PLAIN ANIMAL
4. ROW OF HIGH HILLS
6. TOSS
8. BABY

WORD BANK

BURR	DECORATED	MEAT	BUFFALO
FLICK	RIDGE	CALF	HERD
TIPI	CHIEF	MARRIED	

Name _____   Date _____

TARO YASHIMA

"Crow Boy"

SPECIAL TEST

Chibi was special. We are all special. Answer the questions to the "Special Test." See just how special you are too!

Circle the answer you like best or fill in the blank. Your answers will help you write a short biography of yourself on the back of this page.

1. I like to hum, whistle, or sing.

2. I play an instrument _____.

3. I love to read mysteries, science fiction, adventure, school stories, plays or_____.

4. I like books about real things. My favorite topic is _____.

5. My favorite sport is _____.

6. I like to collect _____.

7. My favorite toy is _____.

8. I couldn't live without my _____.

9. My favorite animal is _____.

10. When I grow up, I'd like to be _____.

11. The thing I like best about my family is _____

_____

Name_____   **Date**_____

DON TORGERSEN

"Huff and Puff and the Troll Hole"

Read "Huff and Puff and the Troll Hole." Use the words in the Word Bank to finish the sentences.

1. _____ went in the troll hole.

2. _____, _____, and _____ were the names of the three trolls.

3. Huff kept his snail in his _____.

4. The trolls let Huff go after he told them he would make _____.

5. Huff and Puff returned the troll eye so they would stop their awful _____.

```
WORD BANK

Bellow      Huff       pocket      soup
Grunt       noise      Roar
```

Now that you know what Don thinks about trolls and gnomes, try to write your own story about some gnomes and trolls. Write your story on a clean piece of paper.

Name_____ Date_____

BERNARD WABER

"Ira Sleeps Over"

Read "Ira Sleeps Over." Use the numbers 1–7 to show the order of the events from the story.

_____ Ira's sister asks if he is taking his teddy bear.

_____ Reggie tells a ghost story.

_____ Ira is invited to sleep over.

_____ Ira decides not to take his teddy bear.

_____ Reggie shows Ira his junk collection.

_____ Ira goes home for his teddy bear.

_____ Reggie gets his teddy bear.

Reread the ghost story that Reggie started to tell Ira. "Once there was this ghost…" Can you finish Reggie's story for him? Use the sheet provided.

Name_____ Date_____

_____ Title

_____

_____

_____

_____

_____

_____

_____

_____

_____

_____

_____

_____

_____

Name_____ **Date**_____

STAN & JAN BERENSTAIN

"Berenstain Bears No Girls Allowed"

Read "The Berenstain Bears No Girls Allowed." Fill in the chart. Put an X on the line under things you think are for boys only, girls only, or for both boys and girls.

	Boy Things	Girl Things	Everybody Things	
running				
jumping rope				
climbing trees				
reading				
cooking				
being in a club				
parties				
having a doll				
having a stuffed animal				
eating				
picking flowers				
helping one another				
cooperating				
loving friends				

Mama Bear said it best, "It doesn't matter if you are a he or a she. Just be the best person you can be."

Name _____   Date _____

ALVIN TRESSELT

"The Mitten"

One day, a little boy lost a mitten. Nine animals tried to keep warm in his mitten. They didn't go into the mitten in alphabetical order. Can you put them in the mitten in alphabetical order?

WORD BANK

MOUSE
FROG
OWL
RABBIT
FOX
WOLF
BOAR
BEAR
CRICKET

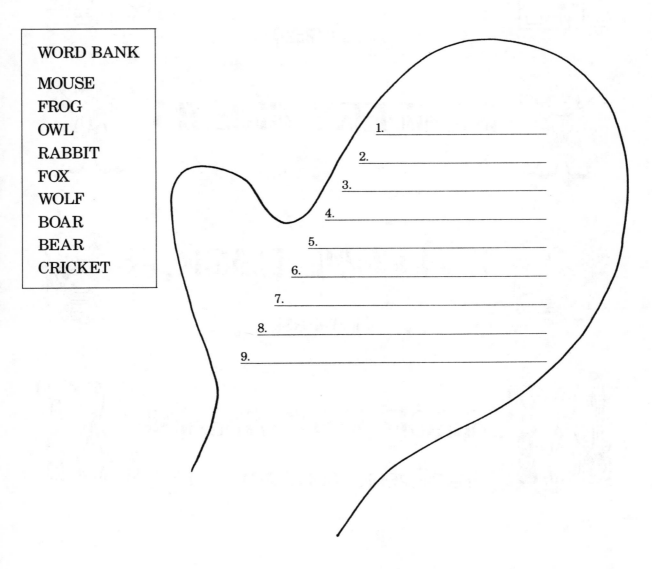

1. _____
2. _____
3. _____
4. _____
5. _____
6. _____
7. _____
8. _____
9. _____

Name _____   Date _____

 # SEPTEMBER

READERS!

 ## WELCOME BACK,

READERS!

 ## READERS ARE #1

 ## WELCOME BACK,

READERS!!

 ## LABOR DAY MEANS

DROP YOUR TOOLS AND READ!!

SEPTEMBER ANSWER KEY

SYD HOFF: *Chester; Julius; Grizzwold*

Chester

1. He wanted the cowboys to take him away.
2. He looked for someone to care for him.
3. He pulled a firetruck, rode on a merry-go-round, and played being a statue.
4. He ran after getting off the merry-go-round.

Julius

1. Julius was lost.
2. Liked to kick a coconut or a football.
3. He sat in a cage at a circus.
4. Davy found him.

Grizzwold

1. He needed a place to live.
2. Liked to fish in the river and sleep outdoors in the forest.
3. He posed for pictures.
4. He found a national park.

ELMER HADER: *The Big Snow*

1. cabbage, tops
2. spring
3. nuts
4. south
5. winter
6. grey, red
7. hollow
8. blanket

ROALD DAHL: *Roald Dahl's Revolting Rhymes*

1. (a) houses of straw, twigs, and bricks; (b) pigs wouldn't let him in; (c) ate the pigs.
2. (a) pigs didn't talk to the wolf, (b) used dynamite on third pig's house; (c) third pig calls Red Riding Hood.

ELSE HOMELUND MINARIK: *Little Bear's Visit*

1. back
2. bear
3. bread
4. come
5. fly
6. free
7. garden
8. hat
9. jam
10. jig
11. kiss
12. nest
13. paws
14. robin
15. sad
16. sang
17. skip
18. sky
19. spring
20. summer
21. toy
22. visit
23. window
24. woods

EDITH THACHER HURD: *Johnny Lion's Bad Day*

1. bad	6. big
2. bed	7. rabbit
3. day	8. cook
4. owl	9. pot
5. eyes	10. kerchew

H.A. REY: *Curious George Visits the Zoo*

1. zoo	6. bananas
2. necks	7. bucket
3. pockets	8. balloon
4. ears/trunks	9. fed
5. animals	10. boy

PAUL GOBLE: *Buffalo Woman*

DON TORGERSEN: *Huff and Puff and the Troll Hole*

1. Huff	4. soup
2. Grunt, Bellow, Roar	5. noise
3. pocket	

BERNARD WABER: *Ira Sleeps Over*

2,5,1,3,4,7,6

ALVIN TRESSELT: *The Mitten*

1. bear	4. fox	7. owl
2. boar	5. frog	8. rabbit
3. cricket	6. mouse	9. wolf

SEPTEMBER AUTHORS BIBLIOGRAPHY

September 2   Bernard Most

If the Dinosaurs Came Back (HBJ, 1978); *My Very Own Dinosaur* (HBJ, 1980); *There's an Ant in Anthony* (Morrow, 1980); *Whatever Happened to the Dinosaurs?* (HBJ, 1984); *Dinosaur Cousins* (HBJ, 1987).

September 3   Aliki Brandenberg

Keep Your Mouth Closed, Dear (Dial, 1966); *Mummies Made in Egypt* (Harper, 1979); *Digging Up Dinosaurs* (Crowell, 1981); *At Mary Bloom's* (Greenwillow, 1983); *Wild & Woolly Mammoths* (Harper, 1983); *Feelings* (Greenwillow, 1984); *Dinosaurs Are Different* (Crowell, 1985); *My Visit to the Dinosaurs* (Harper, 1985); *How a Book Is Made* (Harper, 1986).

September 4   Syd Hoff

Easy-to-read series available in hardcover or paperback and published by Harper: *Albert the Albatross, Barkley, Chester, Danny & the Dinosaur, Grizzwold, Horse in Harry's Room, Little Chief, Oliver, Sammy the Seal, Santa's Moose, Thunderhoof,* and *Where's Prancer?*; *How to Draw Cartoons* (Scholastic, 1975).

September 6   Felix Salten

Bambi: A Life in the Woods (Archway, 1982).

September 7   Elmer Hader

The Big Snow (Macmillan, 1972)—the 1949 Caldecott winner.

September 8   Byron Barton

Crowell Junior Books: *Airplanes, Airport, Trains, Trucks,* and *Wheels; Elephant* (Houghton Mifflin, 1971); *Buzz, Buzz, Buzz* (Macmillan, 1973, out of print); *Hester* (Penguin, 1978); *Building a House* (Penguin, 1984).

September 8   Jack Prelutsky

Nightmares: Poems to Trouble Your Sleep (Greenwillow, 1976); *The Snopp on the Sidewalk & Other Poems* (Greenwillow, 1977); *It's Christmas* (Greenwillow, 1981); *It's Thanksgiving* (Greenwillow, 1982); *It's Valentine's Day* (Greenwillow, 1983); *It's Snowing, It's Snowing* (Greenwillow, 1984); *The New Kid on the Block* (Greenwillow, 1984); *It's Halloween* (Scholastic, 1986); *Ride a Purple Pelican* (Greenwillow, 1986).

September 9   Aileen Fisher

Listen Rabbit (Harper, 1964); *Easter* (Harper, 1968); *Like Nothing at All* (Harper, 1979); *Anybody Home?* (Harper, 1980); *Rabbits, Rabbits* (Harper, 1983).

September Authors Bibliography

September 11   Alfred Slote

My Trip to Alpha I (Avon, 1980); *C.O.L.A.R.* (Lippincott, 1981); *Omega Station* (Lippincott, 1983); *Trouble on Janus* (Lippincott, 1985); *My Robot Buddy* (Harper Trophy, 1986).

September 13   Roald Dahl

Charlie and the Great Glass Elevator (Bantam, 1977); *The Twits* (Bantam, 1982); *Charlie and the Chocolate Factory* (Penguin, 1983); *James and the Giant Peach* (Penguin, 1983); *The Magic Finger* (Harper Junior, 1983); *Dirty Beasts* (Farrar, Straus & Giroux, 1984); *The Enormous Crocodile* (Bantam, 1984); *Roald Dahl's Revolting Rhymes* (Bantam, 1986); *George's Marvelous Medicine* (Bantam, 1987).

September 13   Else Holmelund Minarik

Little Bear series published by Harper: *Little Bear's Visit* (1962 Caldecott winner), *Little Bear, Little Bear's Friend, Kiss for Little Bear, No Fighting, No Biting*.

September 14   Diane Goode (illustrator)

My Little Library of Christmas Classics (Random, 1983); *When I Was Young in the Mountains* (Dutton, 1985); *Watch the Stars Come Out* (Dutton, 1986).

September 14   Edith Thacher Hurd

Last One Home Is a Green Pig (Harper, 1959); *Stop, Stop* (Harper, 1961); *No Funny Business* (Harper, 1962); *Johnny Lion's Book* (Harper, 1965); *Johnny Lion's Bad Day* (Harper, 1970); *Johnny Lion's Rubber Boots* (Harper, 1972).

September 14   John Steptoe

Stevie (Harper, 1963); *Daddy Is a Monster, Sometimes* (Harper, 1980); *Jeffrey Bear Cleans Up His Act* (Lothrop, 1983); *Story of Jumping Mouse* (Lothrop, 1984).

September 14   Robyn Supraner

Troll Associates mysteries: *Case of the Missing Canary, Case of the Missing Rattles, Cat Who Wanted to Fly, The Ghost in the Attic*; I-can-read-about series published by Troll: *Happy Halloween: Things to Make and Do* and *Valentine's Day: Things to Make and Do*.

September 15   Watty Piper

Little Engine That Could (Putnam, 1984).

September 15   Tomie DePaola

Watch Out for the Chicken Feet in Your Soup (Prentice Hall, 1974); *Strega Nona* (Prentice Hall, 1975)—1976 Caldecott Honor book; *Helga's Dowry* (HBJ, 1977); *The Quicksand Book* (Holiday, 1977); *Jamie's Tiger* (HBJ, 1978); *Pancakes for*

Breakfast (HBJ, 1978); *Big Anthony and the Magic Ring* (HBJ, 1979); *The Popcorn Book* (Scholastic, 1979); *Mysterious Giant of Barletta* (HBJ, 1984); *Merry Christmas, Strega Nona* (HBJ, 1986); *Strega Nona's Magic Lessons* (HBJ, 1986); Katie & Kit series published by Simon & Schuster: *Katie & Kit and the Beach, Katie & Kit & Cousin Tom, Katie & Kit & the Sleepover,* and *Katie's Good Idea.*

September 15   Robert McCloskey

Make Way for Ducklings (Viking, 1941)—1942 Caldecott winner; *Blueberries for Sal* (Viking, 1948)—1949 Caldecott Honor book; *One Morning in Maine* (Penguin, 1976).

September 16   Janet Schulman

The Big Hello (Greenwillow, 1976); *Jack the Bum & the Halloween Handout* (Greenwillow, 1977); *Jenny and the Tennis Nut* (Greenwillow, 1978); *Camp Kee Wee's Secret Weapon* (Greenwillow, 1979); *The Great Big Dummy* (Greenwillow, 1979).

September 16   H.A. Rey

Curious George series published by Houghton Mifflin: *Curious George Gets a Medal, CG Learns the Alphabet, CG Rides a Bike, CG Takes a Job;* With Margaret Rey: *CG Goes to the Hospital, CG Flies a Kite;* Margaret Rey editor: *CG & the Dump Truck, CG at the Fire Station, CG Goes Hiking, CG Goes Sledding, CG Goes to the Aquarium, CG Goes to the Circus, CG Visits the Zoo;* Margaret Rey with Allan Shalleck editors: *CG at the Airport, CG at the Ballet, CG at the Laundromat, CG Goes Fishing, CG Goes to a Costume Party, CG Plays Baseball, CG Visits the Police Station, CG Walks the Pets.*

September 17   Paul Goble

The Girl Who Loved Wild Horses (Bradbury, 1978)—1979 Caldecott Award winner; Illustrated many Indian legends for Bradbury Press: *Star Boy* (1983), *Buffalo Woman* (1984), *Gift of the Sacred Dog* (1984), *Death of the Iron Horse* (1987).

September 19   Rachel Field

Hitty: Her First Hundred Years (Macmillan, 1969)—1930 Newbery Award winner; *Prayer for a Child* (Macmillan, 1968)—1945 Caldecott Award winner.

September 21   Taro Yashima

Crow Boy (Viking, 1955)—1956 Caldecott Honor book; *Umbrella* (Penguin, 1977); *Momo's Kitten* (Penguin, 1977).

September 24   Ian Serrailler

Suppose You Met a Witch (Little, Brown, 1973, out of print).

September Authors Bibliography

September 27   Donald Arthur Torgersen

Gnome and Troll series published by Children's Press: *The Girl Who Tricked the Troll, Secret of Cathedral Lake, Last Days of Gorlock the Dragon*.

September 27   Bernard Waber

Just Like Abe Lincoln (Houghton Mifflin, 1964); *Ira Sleeps Over* (Houghton Mifflin, 1972); Lyle the Crocodile series published by Houghton Mifflin: *Funny, Funny Lyle, House on East Eighty Eighth Street, Lovable Lyle, Lyle & the Birthday Party, Lyle Finds His Mother, Lyle, Lyle Crocodile*.

September 29   Stan Berenstain

Berenstain Bear series written with Janice Berenstain published by Random House.

September 30   Edgar D'Aulaire

Abraham Lincoln (Doubleday, 1987)—1940 Caldecott Award winner; other Doubleday titles: *Benjamin Franklin, Columbus, D'Aulaire's Book of Greek Myths, D'Aulaire's Norse Gods and Giants, George Washington*, and *Pocahontas*; *D'Aulaire's Trolls* (Doubleday, 1972—out of print, a fantastic reference for trolls if you can find a copy in your library).

September 30   Alvin Tresselt

Autumn Harvest (Lothrop, 1951); *Frog in the Well* (Lothrop, 1958); *The Mitten* (Lothrop, 1964); *Hide and Seek Fog* (Lothrop, 1965)—1966 Caldecott Honor book.

OCTOBER

OCTOBER AUTHORS

DATE	NAME	AUTHOR	ILLUSTRATOR	K	1	2	3
3	John Carl Himmelman	X			X	X	
3	Molly Cone	X					X
3	Natalie Savage Carlson	X					X
4	Robert Lawson	X	X		X	X	
4	Munro Leaf		X				
4	Donald Sobol	X				X	X
6	Steven Kellogg	X	X	X	X	X	
7	Susan Jeffers		X				
7	Alice Dagliesh	X				X	X
8	Edward Ormondroyd	X				X	X
9	Johanna Hurwitz	X				X	X
10	James Marshall	X	X	X	X	X	X
10	Nancy Carlson	X	X	X	X	X	
14	Miriam Cohen	X		X	X	X	
14	Polly Cameron	X		X	X	X	
16	Noah Webster	Lexicographer					
19	Ed Emberley		X				
20	Crockett Johnson	X	X	X	X	X	
23	Majorie Flack	X			X	X	
24	Bruno Munari	X	X	X	X	X	
28	Leonard Kessler	X	X		X	X	

MUNRO LEAF ROBERT LAWSON

"The Story of Ferdinand"
Author and Illustrator Born on the Same Day!

Read "The Story of Ferdinand." Use the words in the Word Bank to finish the sentences below.

1. Ferdinand lived in _____.

2. All the other little bulls liked to run and _____.

3. Ferdinand liked to smell _____.

4. Ferdinand's favorite tree was a _____ tree.

5. When Ferdinand was older, he sat on a _____. Men looking for bulls thought he was wild.

6. Ferdinand went to Madrid to be in a _____.

7. The matador had a red _____.

8. Ferdinand sat in the bullring and wouldn't _____.

WORD BANK

bee	bullfight	cape	cork
fight	flowers	jump	Spain

Name _____ **Date** _____

DONALD SOBOL

"Encyclopedia Brown, Boy Detective"

Donald Sobol's "Encyclopedia Brown, Boy Detective" is filled with ten short mysteries. If you are going to solve the mysteries with Encyclopedia Brown, you will need to read very carefully. Sobol has a clever way of hiding the clues to solve the mystery. When you read a Sobol mystery, follow these steps:

1. Write the mystery in Box 1.

2. Read the story twice. The details about the place or situation are very important. Look for time clues, weather clues, and fake clues. Write the clues in Box 2 that you think are important.

3. Write the answer to the mystery in Box 3. And read the story again. Does the answer fit the clues from the story?

4. Read the answer to the mystery in the back of the book. If you were right, put a ☆ in Box 4.

If you were wrong put a ☹ in Box 4.

Name _____   Date _____

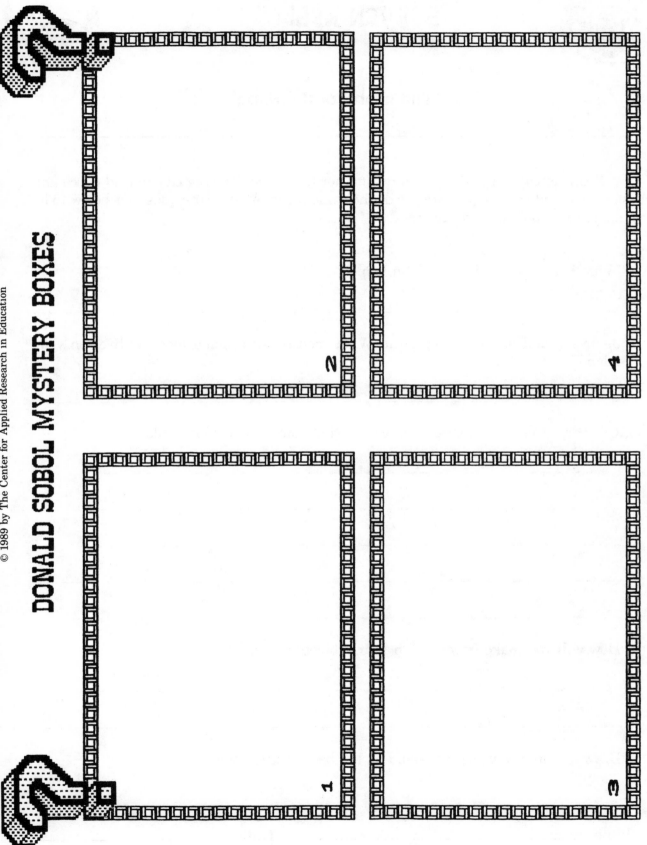

© 1989 by The Center for Applied Research in Education

DONALD SOBOL MYSTERY BOXES

1

2

3

4

STEVEN KELLOGG

"The Island of the Skog"

Read "Island of the Skog." Jenny and her friends left the big city to find peace and safety. Pretend you are planning to do the same thing. Answer the questions below to be prepared for your new adventure.

1. What is the name of your island home.

_____

2. Jenny's island had the Skog on it. What monster or pretend monster lives on your island?

_____

3. Use three to five sentences to describe what your monster looks like:

_____

_____

_____

_____

_____

4. How will you make friends with your problem monster?

_____

_____

5. Draw a map of your secret island on the back of this page.

© 1989 by The Center for Applied Research in Education

Name_____ **Date**_____

JOHANNA HURWITZ

"Busybody Nora"

Read "Busybody Nora." Find the words from the Word Bank in the kettle of stone soup.

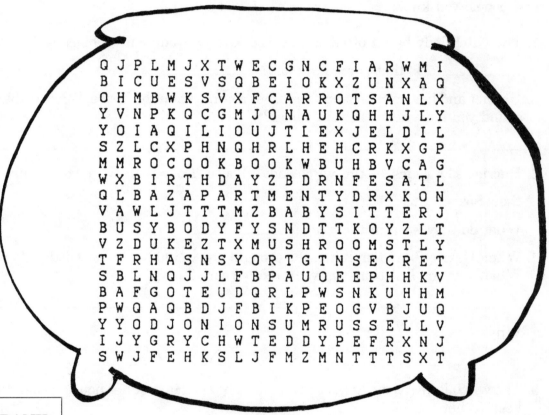

```
Q J P L M J X T W E C G N C F I A R W M I
B I C U E S V S Q B E I O K X Z U N X A Q
O H M B W K S V X F C A R R O T S A N L X
Y V N P K Q C G M J O N A U K Q H H J L Y
Y O I A Q I L I O U J T L E X J E L D I L
S Z L C X P H N Q H R L H E H C R K X G P
M M R O C O O K B O O K W B U H B V C A G
W X B I R T H D A Y Z B D R N F E S A T L
Q L B A Z A P A R T M E N T Y D R X K O N
V A W L J T T M Z B A B Y S I T T E R J
B U S Y B O D Y F Y S N D T T K O Y Z L T
V Z D U K E Z T X M U S H R O O M S T L Y
T F R H A S N S Y O R T G T N S E C R E T
S B L N Q J J L F B P A U O E E P H H K V
B A F G O T E U D Q R L P W S N K U H H M
P W Q A Q B D J F B I K P E O G V B J U Q
Y Y O D J O N I O N S U M R U S S E L L V
I J Y G R Y C H W T E D D Y P E F R X N J
S W J F E H K S L J F M Z M N T T T S X T
```

WORD BANK				
ALLIGATOR	APARTMENT	BABYSITTER	BEANS	BEANSTALK
BIRTHDAY	BUSYBODY	CAKE	CARROTS	COOKBOOK FBI
GIANT	MUSHROOMS	NORA	ONIONS	POTATOES RUSSELL
SECRET	SHERBERT	SCHUBERT	STONESOUP	SURPRISE TEDDY
TOWER				

Name _____   Date _____

NANCY CARLSON

"Louanne Pig in Witch Lady"

Read "Louanne Pig in Witch Lady." Louanne made a very big mistake in this story. She listened to what others said about the Witch Lady. Answer these questions about you and people you know.

1. The witch lady had a black cat. Do you know anyone with a black cat?

   _____ Is that person a witch? _____

2. Harriet and her friends heard screeches coming from the house. What is the strangest sound you have heard in your house?

   _____

3. Harriet saw cages in the witch lady's house. Do you know anyone with a cage in

   their house? _____

   What do they keep in their cage? _____

4. When Harriet hurt her ankle, she thought she would be supper for the old witch lady. When was the last time you were really scared?

   _____

   Why?

   _____

5. The witch lady fixed Harriet's ankle. She showed Harriet her house. What did the lady keep in her cages?

   _____

6. What was the old lady's favorite hobby?

   _____

7. Will Harriet see the witch lady again? _____

   Why? _____

Name _____   Date _____

JAMES MARSHALL

"Yummers"

Read "Yummers!" Emily has a problem with her snacking. The "Bad Snacks" are listed on the left. There are blanks on the right side for "Good Snacks." Can you suggest some "Good Snacks" for Emily from the Word Bank?

BAD SNACKS   GOOD SNACKS

1. tuna fish and jelly   _____

2. buttered corn on the cob   _____

3. eskimo pies   _____

4. cookies   _____

5. vanilla malt   _____

6. banana split   _____

7. pizza   _____

8. cherry pop   _____

9. candied apple   _____

WORD BANK

| juice | apple | frozen yogurt | celery | raisins |
| banana | plain popcorn | skim milk | plain tuna fish | |

Name_____   Date_____

JAMES MARSHALL

"George and Martha"

_____

Read "George and Martha." Martha helps George fix a few problems he has. Use the words in the Word Bank to finish these sentences.

1. George didn't tell Martha that he hated _____.

2. George emptied his supper into his _____.

3. George's flying machine didn't fly because the basket was too _____.

4. George liked to _____ in windows until the day he got a _____ on his head.

5. George put a funny picture of Martha on her _____.

6. When George broke his favorite tooth, the _____

   gave him a _____ one.

```
WORD BANK

bathtub    dentist    gold    heavy    loafers
mirror     peek       split pea soup
```

Name_____   Date_____

MIRIAM COHEN

"The New Teacher"

Read "The New Teacher." Write the words by their meaning. The words in the Word Bank will help you.

1. __ __ __ __   new person

2. __ __ __ __ __   garbage

3. __ __ __ __ __ __   joke

4. __ __ __   gives milk

5. __ __ __ __ __   scream

6. __ __ __ __ __   run after someone

7. __ __ __ __ __ __ __   little cake

8. __ __ __ __   happy

WORD BANK

baby	chase	cow	cupcake
glad	holler	riddle	trash

Name _____   **Date** _____

FALL INTO POEMS IN OCTOBER

**Write a fall poem. Make the first word of each line start with the
same letter as the words Fall, Autumn, Leaf, Pumpkin, or Harvest.
Try your best. Use the example below for help.**

FALLEN LEAVES
ARE ALWAYS
LOVLIEST
LYING IN A HEAP!

Name _____ **Date** _____

NOAH WEBSTER

Lexicographer—Writer of Definitions

Noah Webster lived from 1758 to 1843. That was a very long time ago. In his day, people sometimes didn't know how other people used certain words. Can you imagine wanting a dog for your birthday, and mom and dad buy you a cat?

Understanding words is important. But let's be silly. Let's define words as something else. Read the examples and see if you can be a lexicographer (writer of definitions), even if they are silly.

EXAMPLES OF STRANGE BIRDS

Baseball buzzard: perches on baseball benches and watches baseball games. It is very similar to the football buzzard. However, most football buzzards hang around couches on Sunday afternoons and Monday nights.

Kiddie Hawk: Adult Kiddie Hawks are found in schools watching children. They are very fond of children. Sometimes they do cause children to be unhappy when they tell them to do homework:

1. Define these strange birds:

Tennis Turkey:

_____

_____

_____

Story Sparrow:

_____

_____

_____

2. Name some more strange birds and write definitions for them:

_____

_____

_____

_____

Name _____   Date _____

ED EMBERLEY

"The Great Thumbprint Drawing Book"

Look at all the pictures Ed Emberley has drawn in "The Great Thumbprint Drawing Book." Here are some thumb and finger-prints for you. Add lines, wiggles, and swiggles. Turn them into animals, faces, and things. The first frame is a set of examples for you.

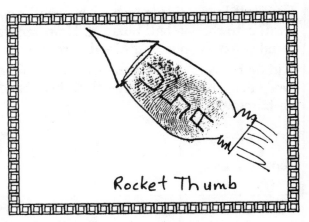

Name _____ **Date** _____

CROCKETT JOHNSON

"A Picture for Harold's Room"

Read "A Picture for Harold's Room." Get a purple crayon and draw your own wonderful picture.

Name_____ **Date**_____

MARJORIE FLACK

"Story About Ping"

Read "Story About Ping." Use the words in the Word Bank to write the words that match their meanings on the right.

1. __ __ __ __ __ __   crosses water

2. __ __ __ __   floats on water

3. __ __ __ __   lives in the water

4. __ __ __ __   edge of land by water

5. __ __ __ __   move through water

6. __ __ __ __ __ __   kick feet in water

7. __ __ __ __   duck's mouth

8. __ __ __ __ __ __   color of Ping

9. __ __ __ __ __   arms of a duck

10. __ __ __ __ __ __ __   what Ping got

WORD BANK

bank	bill	boat	bridge	fish
paddle	spanked	swim	wings	yellow

Name_____   Date_____

LEONARD KESSLER

"Old Turtle's Baseball Stories"

Read "Old Turtle's Baseball Stories." Use the words in the Word Bank to finish these sentences.

1. In the summer, the friends played _____.

2. In the winter, they told each other _____.

3. _____ was the greatest pitcher.

4. She threw _____ balls at the same time.

5. Later, she sold _____.

6. _____ was the greatest hitter.

7. He hit the ball with his _____.

8. Carla Kangaroo was the best _____.

9. Her _____ caught a flyball one time to save the game.

10. _____ tells the best stories.

WORD BANK				
antlers	baseball	four	hot dogs	joey
moose	octopus	outfielder	stories	turtle

Name_____ Date_____

COLUMBUS DAY

OCTOBER
READERS

OCTOBER

TRICK OR TREAT

OCTOBER

GRANDPARENTS' DAY

HAPPY HAUNTING

OCTOBER

HAPPY HAUNTING

OCTOBER ANSWER KEY

MUNRO LEAF AND ROBERT LAWSON: *The Story of Ferdinand*

1. Spain
2. jump
3. flowers
4. cork

5. bee
6. bullfight
7. cape
8. fight

JOHANNA HURWITZ: *Busybody Nora*

```
Q J P L M J X T W E C G N C F I A R W M I
B I C U E S V S Q B E I O K X Z U N X A Q
O H M B W K S V X F C A R R O T S A N L X
Y V N P K Q C G M J O N A U K Q H H J L Y
Y O I A Q I L I O U J T L E X J E L D I L
S Z L C X P H N Q H R L H E H C R K X G P
M M R O C O O K B O O K W B U H B V C A G
W X B I R T H D A Y Z B D R N F E S A T L
Q L B A Z A P A R T M E N T Y D R X K O N
V A W L J T T T M Z B A B Y S I T T E R J
B U S Y B O D Y F Y S N D T T K O Y Z L T
V Z D U K E Z T X M U S H R O O M S T L Y
T F R H A S N S Y O R T G T N S E C R E T
S B L N Q J J L F B P A U O E E P H H K V
B A F G O T E U D Q R L P W S N K U H H M
P W Q A Q B D J F B I K P E O G V B J U Q
Y Y O D J O N I O N S U M R U S S E L L V
I J Y G R Y C H W T E D D Y P E F R X N J
S W J F E H K S L J F M Z M N T T T S X T
```

JAMES MARSHALL: *Yummers*

1. plain tuna fish
2. plain popcorn
3. frozen yogurt
4. raisins (answers could vary)
5. skim milk

6. banana
7. celery (answers could vary)
8. juice
9. apple

JAMES MARSHALL: *George and Martha*

1. split pea soup
2. loafers
3. heavy

4. peek; bathtub
5. mirror
6. dentist; gold

45

October Answer Key

MIRIAM COHEN: *The New Teacher*

1. baby
2. trash
3. riddle
4. cow

5. holler
6. chase
7. cupcake
8. glad

MAJORIE FLACK: *Story About Ping*

1. bridge
2. boat
3. fish
4. bank
5. swim

6. paddle
7. bill
8. yellow
9. wings
10. spanked

LEONARD KESSLER: *Old Turtle's Baseball Stories*

1. baseball
2. stories
3. octopus
4. four
5. hot dogs

6. moose
7. antlers
8. outfielder
9. joey
10. turtle

OCTOBER AUTHORS BIBLIOGRAPHY

October 3   John Carl Himmelman

Talestar the Lizard (Dial, 1982); *The Talking Tree* (Viking, 1986); *Amanda & the Magic Garden* (Viking, 1987); *Amanda & the Witch Switch* (Viking, date not set).

October 3   Molly Cone

Mishmash (Archway, 1971); series published by Houghton Mifflin: *Mishmash & the Big Fat Problem, Mishmash & the Robot, Mishmash & the Sauerkraut,* and *Mishmash & the Substitute Teacher.*

October 3   Natalie Savage Carlson

Empty Schoolhouse (Harper, 1965); *Spooky Night* (Lothrop, 1982); series: *Spooky & the Wizard's Bats, Spooky and the Ghost Cat, Ghost in the Lagoon;* Orpheline series published by Dell: *Happy Orpheline, Grandmother for the Orphelines, Brother for the Orphelines.*

October 4   Robert Lawson

They Were Strong and Good (Viking, 1940)—1941 Caldecott Award winner; *Rabbit Hill* (Viking, 1944)—1945 Newbery Award winner; illustrated *The Story of Ferdinand* by Munro Leaf (Penguin, 1977); *The Tough Winter* (Penguin, 1979); *Captain Kidd's Cat* (Little, Brown, 1984).

October 4   Munro Leaf

Safety Can Be Fun (Lippincott, 1961, revised); *Metric Can Be Fun* (Lippincott, 1976); *The Story of Ferdinand* (Penguin, 1977); *Manners Can Be Fun* (Lippincott, 1985).

October 4   Donald Sobol

Encyclopedia Brown series now in Bantam paperback, Scholastic paperback, and Morrow Junior Books hardcover.

October 6   Steven Kellogg

Pinkerton series published by Dial: *Pinkerton Behave, Prehistoric Pinkerton, A Rose for Pinkerton, Tallyho Pinkerton; The Island of the Skog* (Dial, 1973); *Can I Keep Him?* (Dial, 1976); *Much Bigger Than Martin* (Dial, 1976); *Won't Somebody Play With Me* (Dial, 1976); *Mysterious Tadpole* (Dial, 1977); *Ralph's Secret Weapon* (Dial, 1986).

October 7   Susan Jeffers

Three Jovial Huntsmen (Bradbury, 1973)—1974 Caldecott Honor book; *Wild Robin* (Dutton, 1976); *Hansel and Gretel* (Dial, 1980); *Snow Queen* (Dial, 1982); *All the Pretty Horses* (Scholastic, 1985); *Wild Swans* (Dial, 1987).

October Authors Bibliography

October 7 Alice Dalgliesh

The Courage of Sarah Noble (Scribner, 1954); *Thanksgiving Story* (Scribner, 1954); *Columbus Story*, Illustrated by Leo Politi (Scribner, 1955).

October 8 Edward Ormondroyd

Broderick (Houghton Mifflin, 1969); *Theodore* (Houghton Mifflin, 1984); *Theodore's Rival* (Houghton Mifflin, 1986).

October 9 Johanna Hurwitz

All books published by Morrow Junior Books: *Busybody Nora* (1976); *Baseball Fever* (1981); *Nora and Mrs. Mind-Your-Own-Business* (1982); *Tough-Luck Karen* (1982); *Rip-roaring Russel* (1983); *DeDe Takes Charge* (1984); *Hot and Cold Summer* (1984); *Adventures of Ali Babba Bernstein* (1985); *Russell Rides Again* (1985); *Russell Sprouts* (1987); Aldo series: *Much Ado About Aldo* (1978), *Aldo Applesauce* (1979), *Aldo Ice Cream* (1981).

October 10 Nancy Carlson

All books published by Carolrhoda Books: Harriet series, Loudmouth George series, Louanne Pig series; *Bunnies and Their Hobbies* (1984); *Bunnies and Their Sports* (1987).

October 10 James Marshall

George and Martha series published by Houghton Mifflin: *One Fine Day, Back in Town, Encore, Rise and Shine, Tons of Fun*; *Yummers* (Houghton Mifflin, 1973); *Taking Care of Carruthers* (Houghton Mifflin, 1981); *Yummers Too* (Houghton Mifflin, 1985); *What's the Matter with Carruthers?* (Houghton Mifflin, 1987); collaborator and illustrator for Miss Nelson series by Harry Allard; *Merry Christmas Space Case* (Dial, 1986); *The Cut-Ups* (Viking Kestrel, 1987); *The Cut-Ups Cut Loose* (Viking Kestrel, 1987); as Edward Marshal: *Space Case* (Dial, 1980); *Fox & His Friends* (Dial, 1982); *Fox in Love* (Dial, 1982); *Fox at School* (Dial, 1983); *Fox on Wheels* (Dial, 1983); *Four on the Shore* (Dial, 1985).

October 14 Miriam Cohen

First grade series published by Greenwillow: *First Grade Takes a Test, Lost in the Museum, The New Teacher, No Good in Art, Starring First Grade, When Will I Read*; *Best Friends* (Macmillan, 1971); *Bee My Valentine* (Greenwillow, 1978); *Jim Meets the Thing* (Greenwillow, 1981); *Jim's Dog Muffins* (Greenwillow, 1984).

October 14 Polly Cameron

I Can't Said the Ant (original publisher Coward McCann, reprinted by Scholastic, 1961—out of print).

October 16 Noah Webster

Compiler of world-famous dictionary.

October Authors Bibliography

October 19 Ed Emberley

Illustrator of *Drummer Hoff* (Prentice Hall, 1967)—1968 Caldecott Award winner, with text written by Barbara Emberley; drawing books by the dozen published by Little, Brown & Company: *Big Purple Drawing Book, Big Green Drawing Book, Big Orange Drawing Book, Big Red Drawing Book, Make a World, Drawing Book of Animals, Drawing Book of Faces, Circle Pie, Great Thumbprint Drawing Book.*

October 20 Crockett Johnson

Will Spring Be Early or Late? (Crowell, 1959); Harold and his purple crayon series published by Harper Junior: *Picture for Harold's Room* (1960), *Harold and the Purple Crayon* (1981), *Harold's Circus* (1981), *Harold's Trip to the Sky* (1981).

October 23 Majorie Flack

Angus and the Ducks (Doubleday, 1930); *Story About Ping* (Viking 1933); Ask Mr. Bear (Macmillan, 1986).

October 24 Bruno Munari

Bruno Munari's ABC (World, 1960); *Bruno Munari's Zoo* (World, 1963—out of print).

October 28 Leonard Kessler

Last One in Is a Rotten Egg (Harper, 1969); *Old Turtle's Baseball Stories* (Greenwillow, 1982); *Big Mile Race* (Greenwillow, 1983); *Old Turtle's Winter Games* (Greenwillow, 1983); *Old Turtle's Riddle and Joke Book* (Greenwillow, 1986).

NOVEMBER

November 4	Gail Haley, *Jack and the Fire Dragon* (fill in)
November 8	Marianna Mayer, *The Black Horse* (special friend questions)
	Marianna Mayer, *The Unicorn and the Lake* (fill in)
November 12	Marjorie Sharmat, *Nate the Great and the Snowy Trail* (five mystery words)
November 13	Robert Louis Stevenson, "Rain," "Time to Rise," "Bed in Summer" (writing poems)
November 14	Miska Miles, *Annie and the Old One* (word meanings)
November 14	William Steig, *Sylvester and the Magic Pebble* (writing activity)
November 14	Astrid Lindgren, *Christmas in Noisy Village* (fill in/Christmas customs)
November 15	Daniel Pinkwater, *I Was a Second Grade Werewolf* (three whys)
November 24	Mordicai Gerstein, *Prince Sparrow* (fill in)
November 25	Marc Brown, *Arthur's Thanksgiving* (fill in)
	Marc Brown, *Pickle Things* (writing activity)
November 28	Tomi Ungerer, *The Three Robbers* (fill in)
November 30	Margot Zemach, *It Could Always Be Worse* (short, thankful answers)

November Bookmarks
November Answer Key
November Authors Bibliography

NOVEMBER AUTHORS

DATE	NAME	AUTHOR/ILLUSTRATOR		READING LEVEL			
				K	1	2	3
1	Fred Neff	X					X
2	Margaret Bloy Graham		X	X	X	X	
4	Gail Haley	X	X				
8	Marianna Mayer	X	X			X	X
10	Kate Seredy	X	X	X	X		
12	Marjorie Sharmat	X		X	X	X	
13	Nathaniel Benchley	X		X	X	X	
13	Robert Louis Stevenson	X		X	X	X	
14	Astrid Lindgren	X		X	X	X	
14	Alan Baker	X	X	X	X		
14	Miska Miles	X				X	X
14	William Steig	X	X	X	X	X	X
15	Daniel Pinkwater	X				X	X
16	Edna Walker Chandler	X			X	X	
16	Jean Fritz	X					X
19	Margaret Musgrove	X				X	X
21	Leo Politi	X				X	X
23	Marc Simont		X				
24	Carlo Collodi	X					X
24	Mordicai Gerstein	X	X			X	X
25	Marc Brown	X	X	X	X	X	
26	Charles Schulz	X	X	PEANUTS IS FOR EVERYONE!			
28	Stephanie Calmenson	X				X	X
28	Tomi Ungerer	X	X			X	X
30	Margot Zemach	X	X			X	X

GAIL HALEY

"Jack and the Fire Dragon"

Read "Jack and the Fire Dragon." Use the words in the Word Bank to finish these sentences about Jack's brave adventure.

1. Poppyseed loves to tell _____.

2. Old Fire Dragaman was a fierce _____.

3. Jack and his _____ went to clear the land for a new home.

4. Tom was a good _____.

5. His dinner woke up old _____ Dragaman.

6. The nasty giant ate Will's _____.

7. Jack followed Old Fire Dragaman to his _____.

8. Jack's brothers wanted the _____.

9. Jenny gave Jack a magic _____.

10. Jack killed the dragon with a magic _____.

11. He found the gold and _____ himself home.

12. Late at night, you can still see _____ over Brown's Mountain.

WORD BANK

brothers	cave	cook	fire	fireballs	giant
ring	stories	sword	treasure	turkey	wished

Name _____   Date _____

MARIANNA MAYER

"The Black Horse"

Read "The Black Horse." This story points out the true value of a friendship, what can I do for you rather than what can you do for me. Giving is not just an idea for Christmas. Answer the questions below to help you learn about your best friend.

1. Who is your special friend?

   _____

2. Can you name three things your friend likes to do?

   _____

   _____

   _____

3. What was the last thing that you did for your friend when he or she really needed help?

   _____

   _____

   _____

4. When friends argue, it's important to say "I'm sorry." When was the last time you had to say "I'm sorry"?

   _____

   _____

Name _____   **Date** _____

MARIANNA MAYER

"The Unicorn and the Lake"

Read "The Unicorn and the Lake." Marianna Mayer did not draw the pictures for her story about the unicorn. But Michael Hague did do an excellent job for her! Use the words in the Word Bank to complete the sentences about the magical unicorn.

1. Long ago, all animals _____ one language.

2. The unicorn _____ in the lower lands.

3. Hunters wanted the unicorn's _____ for its magic.

4. He escaped to the _____.

5. He took his _____ with him.

6. The animals _____ how to talk to one another.

7. They shared a _____.

8. But with no rain, it became _____.

9. The animals cried for _____ under the moon.

10. The unicorn pierced the _____ with his horn.

11. The _____ poisoned the lake.

12. The unicorn _____ it.

13. The unicorn made the lake _____ again.

WORD BANK				
clouds	forest	forgot	horn	killed
lake	lived	magic	mountains	pure
rain	serpent	shallow	spoke	talk

© 1989 by The Center for Applied Research in Education

Name_____ Date_____

MARJORIE SHARMAT

Read "Nate the Great and the Snowy Trail"

Read "Nate the Great and the Snowy Trail." Answer the questions about the Five Mystery words.

1. Who asked Nate the Great to solve the mystery?

_____

2. What was Nate supposed to find?

_____

3. What clues did Nate collect?

_____

_____

_____

_____

4. When did Nate find his last clue?

_____

5. Where did Nate discover the last clue?

_____

6. Why didn't Nate like his birthday present?

_____

Name_____ **Date**_____

ROBERT LOUIS STEVENSON

"A Child's Garden of Verses"

Read the following poems by Robert Louis Stevenson. He put childhood memories so neatly into words and lines that rhyme.

Rain

The rain is raining all around,
It falls on field and tree
It falls on the umbrellas here,
And on ships at sea.

text from *A Child's Garden of Verses* Macmillan, 1927

Time to Rise

A birdie with a yellow bill
Hopped upon the window sill,
Cocked his shining eye and said:
"Ain't you ashamed, you sleepy-head!

text from *A Child's Garden of Verses* Macmillan, 1927

Bed in Summer

In winter I get up at night
And dress by yellow candle light.
In summer, quite the other way,
I have to go to bed by day.

I have to go to bed and see
The birds still hopping on the tree,
Or hear the grown-up people's feet
Still going past me on the street.

And does it not seem hard to you,
When all the sky is clear and blue,
And I should like so much to play,
To have to go to bed by day

text from *A Child's Garden of Verses* Macmillan, 1927

ROBERT LOUIS STEVENSON

"A Child's Garden of Verses"

The poems printed below are modeled on "Rain" by Robert Louis Stevenson. Fill in the blank lines to create a new poem.

SNOW

The snow is snowing all around,

Falling on the streets and _____.

Out the door I leap with a _____,

to make a snowball cold and _____.

To solve this poem, think of words that rhyme with "around."

Try another poem about HALE

The hale is haling all around,

Klunking cars up and down the street.

Out the door I leap, but slip from my _____,

And end up looking at the hale on the _____.

Now try the SUN

The sun is _____ all around,

Making my ice cream drip to the _____.

I'm glad it's not the last Mom _____,

But I'll need to find some _____.

What other poems can you think of to fit these four lines? Try your best. Robert Louis Stevenson would be proud of you!!

_____

_____

_____

_____

Name_____ **Date**_____

© 1989 by The Center for Applied Research in Education

MISKA MILES

"Annie and the Old One"

Read "Annie and the Old One." Miska Miles wrote a beautiful story about the love of a granddaughter for her grandmother. When the Old One tells everyone she will return to Mother Earth when the weaving is finished, she asks each to name a gift. Annie picks her weaving stick, but sets out to make sure the weaving is not finished. When every attempt fails, she talks with the Old One. In the end, Annie understands that everything lives and dies. It is a part of nature.

Below is a list of words used in "Annie and the Old One." Match the word to its definition.

1. _____ to feed on growing grass

2. _____ small section of raised land with steep sides

3. _____ earth-walled hut

4. _____ tufts at the top of a corn plant

5. _____ frame that holds a weaving

6. _____ a desert plant

7. _____ to make by interlacing thread or yarn

8. _____ bringing in crops when they are ready

9. _____ yarn from sheep hair

10. _____ orange-yellow gourd with many seeds

11. _____ coarsely ground corn, used like flour

WORD BANK

| cactus | graze | harvesting | hogan | loom | meal |
| mesa | pumpkin | tassels | weave | wool | |

Name_____   Date_____

WILLIAM STEIG

"Sylvester and the Magic Pebble"

Read "Sylvester and the Magic Pebble." In this story, you learn magic can be a tricky thing. At the end, Sylvester and his parents "put the magic pebble in an iron safe." They thought they might want to use it someday.

That day is today! Sylvester has a problem. Answer the questions below to help you write a story, "Magic Pebble II."

1. Sylvester needs _____.

2. But he doesn't have any _____.

3. He asks his father to use the pebble. Dad says no. How will Sylvester get the pebble?

_____

_____

_____

4. When Sylvester makes his wish, what goes wrong this time?

_____

_____

_____

5. How is Sylvester saved?

_____

_____

_____

Name _____ **Date** _____

ASTRID LINDGREN

"Christmas in Noisy Village"

Read "Christmas in Noisy Village." Astrid Lindgren tells us how children spend the days before Christmas. Fill in the blanks to learn more about the Christmas customs in Sweden.

1. Children put sheaves of _____ out to feed hungry sparrows.

2. Three days before Christmas, they bake _____ cookies.

3. They gather _____ for the fireplaces.

4. They cut down their own Christmas _____.

5. They sing _____ by the houses of their friends.

6. They make snow _____ by piling snowballs around lighted _____.

7. They _____ their trees with _____.

8. They eat lots of _____ and _____.

9. They sing "_____ Night, _____ Night."

10. They wait for Santa Claus to bring the _____.

Put a circle around the number of the sentences that you do just like Swedish children.

WORD BANK

apples	candles	carols	decorate	firewood
gingersnap	ham	holy	lanterns	oats
presents	sausage	silent	trees	

Name_____   Date_____

DANIEL PINKWATER

"I Was a Second Grade Werewolf"

Read "I Was a Second Grade Werewolf." Pinkwater wrote a very strange story. Answer the WHY-WHY-WHY questions below.

1. Why didn't anyone see a difference in the second grader?

_____

_____

2. Why did he run on all fours, bite the little girl, and bend the iron bars?

_____

_____

3 Why did the little boy change back to normal?

_____

_____

4. If you woke up as a creature tomorrow, what would you be?

_____

5. What would you do? _____

_____

_____

_____

Name_____ **Date**_____

MORDICAI GERSTEIN

"Prince Sparrow"

Read "Prince Sparrow." Mordicai's story shows that even a princess can be a brat as well as a queen. Use the words from the Word Bank to finish the sentences.

1. A _____ princess was _____ and _____ to her maids.

2. She was _____ to her tutor.

3. If she didn't get what she wanted, she threw a _____.

4. She wanted to be a _____ when she grew up. Then she could turn anyone

   into a _____.

5. One day a _____ flew into her room.

6. She thought it was a _____ under a magic _____.

7. She had a _____ cage made for it.

8. It ate her _____ and made her _____.

9. One day, the sparrow wanted to be _____.

10. But he came back to live with the princess who grew into a sweet _____.

```
WORD BANK
free          laugh         mean          nasty         prince        queen         rude
selfish       silver        sparrow       spell         strawberries
tantrum       toad          witch
```

Name_____ **Date**_____

MARC BROWN

"Arthur's Thanksgiving"

Read "Arthur's Thanksgiving." Use the Word Bank below to fill in the sentences.

1. Arthur wanted to be the _____ of the school play.

2. Francine thought it would be a _____.

3. Arthur's first job was to assign _____.

4. _____ wanted to be the narrator.

5. She had the loudest _____.

6. Muffy had braids. She wanted to be the Indian _____.

7. No one wanted to be the _____.

8. In 1620, Pilgrims sailed to America on the _____.

9. When we think of _____, we think of a turkey.

10. _____ was brave enough to be the turkey.

© 1989 by The Center for Applied Research in Education

WORD BANK

Arthur	director	disaster	Francine	Mayflower
parts	princess	Thanksgiving	turkey	voice

Name_____   Date_____

MARC BROWN

"Pickle Things"

Read "Pickle Things." "Pickle Things" is a silly story about all the ways we don't use pickles. Pick something else and make a silly story. Try your best to make it rhyme. Draw pictures to go with it. Here is one idea for you to think about.

Marshmallow things you never see,

like a marshmallow boat in a chocolate sea.

A marshmallow ring,

a marshmallow rose,

and marshmallow clothes

or marshmallow bows.

A marshmallow car,

or a marshmallow bus.

What's all this marshmallow fuss.

I'd like a marshmallow over a fire, on a stick;

spread between graham crackers and chocolate—

oh so thick.

A marshmallow is never so great

as when it's simply ate!

NOW IT'S YOUR TURN!! Write your story on the back of this page.

Name_____ Date_____

TOMI UNGERER

"The Three Robbers"

Read "The Three Robbers." Use the words from the Word Bank to fill in these sentences.

1. Once upon a time, there were three _____.

2. They wore black hats and _____.

3. They used an _____, a pepper-_____, and a _____ to steal from people.

4. They lived in a cave high in the _____.

5. They had _____ full of _____.

6. One night, they stopped a _____ that had one passenger, an _____ named Tiffany.

7. They built a _____ for unhappy and abandoned children.

8. The children dressed in red _____ and capes.

9. When the children grew and married, they built _____ near their robbers.

10. They built three _____ to remember their foster fathers.

```
WORD BANK
ax          blower      blunderbuss   capes     carriage
castle      gold        hats          houses    mountains
orphan      robbers     towers        trunks
```

Name_____   Date_____

© 1989 by The Center for Applied Research in Education

MARGOT ZEMACH

"It Could Always Be Worse"

Read "It Could Always Be Worse." When the peasant in the story lets all the animals out of his small hut, he knows how lucky he is. He is very human. Just like us, he thought he had it worse than anyone.

This is a good month to think about being thankful. Answer these questions to prepare a letter to mom and dad telling them how thankful you are. Write your letter neatly on a clean piece of paper.

1. Why are you thankful for your house? Is it big, just right, small but happy?

_____

2. How can you say you're thankful for healthy brothers and sisters? If they aren't perfectly healthy, how are you happy to know them?

_____

3. In what ways are you thankful for mom and dad?

_____

4. Is there anyone at school (teacher or friend) you are especially thankful for? In what way?

_____

5. I am thankful for kids who listen and great books to read. Can you name three people or things you are thankful for? List a short reason for each.

_____

_____

_____

Name_____ **Date**_____

 **NOVEMBER**
READERS!

 **NOVEMBER**

 **NOVEMBER**

WE'RE THANKFUL FOR BOOKS!

 **NOVEMBER**

NOVEMBER ANSWER KEY

GAIL HALEY: *Jack and the Fire Dragon*

1. stories
2. giant
3. brothers
4. cook
5. fire
6. turkey
7. cave
8. treasure
9. ring
10. sword
11. wished
12. fireballs

MARIANNA MAYER: *The Unicorn and the Lake*

1. spoke
2. lived
3. horn
4. mountains
5. magic
6. forgot
7. lake
8. shallow
9. rain
10. clouds
11. serpent
12. killed
13. pure; forest

MARJORIE SHARMAT: *Nate the Great and the Snowy Trail*

1. Rosamond
2. His early birthday present
3. The present was heavy; was small enough to fit on a sled; footprints of Rosamond in the snow; Rosamond thought it was a most beautiful present
4. When he thought about Sludge leaping in the snow
5. By the tree
6. Nate doesn't like cats

ROBERT LOUIS STEVENSON: *A Child's Garden of Verses*

Answers may vary

1. ground; all around
   bound
   round
2. feet
   street
3. shining
   ground
   made
   shade

November Answer Key

MISKA MILES: *Annie and the Old One*

1. graze
2. mesa
3. hogan
4. tassels
5. loom
6. cactus
7. weave
8. harvesting
9. wool
10. pumpkin
11. meal

ASTRID LINDGREN: *Christmas in Noisy Village*

1. oats
2. gingersnap
3. firewood
4. trees
5. carols
6. lanterns; candles
7. decorate; apples
8. ham; sausage
9. silent; holy
10. presents

DANIEL PINKWATER: *I Was a Second Grade Werewolf*

1. Because he didn't know how to behave
2. He was pretending
3. Because he wasn't getting any attention
4. Answers will vary
5. Answers will vary

MORDICAI GERSTEIN: *Prince Sparrow*

1. selfish; mean; nasty
2. rude
3. tantrum
4. witch; toad
5. sparrow
6. prince; spell
7. silver
8. strawberries; laugh
9. free
10. queen

MARC BROWN: *Arthur's Thanksgiving*

1. director
2. disaster
3. parts
4. Francine
5. voice
6. princess
7. turkey
8. Mayflower
9. Thanksgiving
10. Arthur

TOMI UNGERER: *The Three Robbers*

1. robbers
2. capes
3. ax; blower; blunderbuss
4. mountains
5. trunks; gold
6. carriage; orphan
7. castle
8. hats
9. houses
10. towers

NOVEMBER AUTHORS BIBLIOGRAPHY

November 1   Fred Neff

All titles available from Lerner Publications for third graders who love reading about combative sports: *Basic Jujitsu Handbook, Basic Karate Handbook, Basic Self-Defense Handbook, Hand-Fighting Manual, Karate Is for Me, Keeping Fit Handbook for Physical Conditioning and Better Health.*

November 2   Margaret Bloy Graham

Wrote and illustrated: *Be Nice to Spiders* (Harper, 1967); *Benjy and the Barking Bird* (Harper, 1971); *Benjy's Dog House* (Harper, 1973); *Benjy's Boat Trip* (Harper, 1977); illustrated Gene Zion's series: *Harry the Dirty Dog, No Roses for Harry, Harry and the Lady Next Door.*

November 4   Gail Haley

A Story, A Story (Macmillan, 1970)—1971 Caldecott Award winner; *Birdsong* (Crown, 1984); *Jack and the Bean Tree* (Crown, 1986); *Jack and the Fire Dragon* (Crown, 1988).

November 8   Marianna Mayer

Beauty and the Beast (Macmillan, 1978); *The Unicorn and the Lake* (Dial, 1982); *The Black Horse* (Dial, 1984); *Aladdin and the Enchanted Lamp* (Macmillan, 1985); *Alley Oop!* (Holt, 1985); *Little Jewel Box* (Dial, 1986); *The Twelve Dancing Princesses* (Morrow, 1986); *Ugly Duckling* (Macmillan, 1987).

November 10   Kate Seredy

The White Stag (Penguin, 1979); *Good Master* (Penguin, 1986).

November 12   Marjorie Sharmat

This prolific author writes for every grade from kindergarten through junior high: Nate the Great mystery series published by Dell; *Goodnight Andrew, Goodnight Craig* (Harper, 1969); *A Big, Fat, Enormous Lie* (Dutton, 1978); *Gila Monsters Meet You at the Airport* (Macmillan, 1980); *Attila the Angry* (Holiday, 1985).

November 13   Nathaniel Benchley

All published by Harper: *Red Fox and His Canoe* (1964); *Oscar Otter* (1966); *Sam the Minuteman* (1969); *Several Tricks of Edgar Dolphin* (1970); *Small Wolf* (1972); *A Ghost Named Fred* (1979); *Strange Disappearance of Arthur Cluck* (1979); *Walter the Homing Pigeon* (1981); *George the Drummer Boy* (1987).

November Authors Bibliography

November 13   Robert Louis Stevenson

A Child's Garden of Verses (Golden Press, 1951, illustrated by Alice and Martin Provensen—out of print); *A Child's Garden of Verses* (Putnam, 1957); *A Child's Garden of Verses* (Macmillan, 1981).

November 14   Alan Baker

Benjamin (hamster) series: *Benjamin Bounces Back* (Lippincott, 1978); *Benjamin's Dreadful Dream* (Lippincott, 1980); *Benjamin's Book* (Lothrop, 1983); *Benjamin's Portrait* (Lothrop, 1986).

November 14   Miska Miles

Annie and the Old One (Little, Brown, 1971)—1972 Newberry Honor book; *Small Rabbit* (Scholastic, 1981); *Gertrude's Pocket* (Peter Smith, 1984).

November 14   William Steig

Roland the Minstrel Pig (Harper, 1968); author/illustrator of *Sylvester and the Magic Pebble* (Windmill Books/Simon & Schuster, 1969)—1970 Caldecott Award winner; *Dominic* (Farrar, 1972); *Abel's Island* (Farrar, 1976); *Amazing Bone* (Farrar, 1976); *Doctor DeSoto* (Farrar, 1982); *Brave Irene* (Farrar, 1986).

November 14   Astrid Lindgren

Children of Noisy Village (Viking, 1962); *The Tomten* (Putnam, 1979); *The Tomten and the Fox* (Putnam, 1979); *Christmas in Noisy Village* (Penguin, 1981); Pippi Longstocking fantasy series: *Pippi Goes on Board, Pippi in the South Seas, Pippi Longstocking, Pippi on the Run.*

November 15   Daniel Pinkwater

Fat Men from Space (Dodd, 1977); *The Hoboken Chicken Emergency* (Prentice Hall, 1977); *Attila the Pun* (Macmillan, 1981); *I Was a Second Grade Werewolf* (Dutton, 1983).

November 16   Edna Walker Chandler

Cowboy Andy (Random, 1959); *Five Cent, Five Cent* (Whitman, 1967).

November 16   Jean Fritz

All published by Putnam: *And Then What Happened, Paul Revere?* (1973); *Where Was Patrick Henry on the 29th of May?* (1975); *Who's That Stepping on Plymouth Rock?* (1975); *Will You Sign Here, John Hancock?* (1976); *Where Do You Think You're Going, Christopher Columbus?* (1980); *What's the Big Idea, Ben Franklin?* (1982); *Why Don't You Get a Horse, Sam Adams?* (1982); *Can't You Make Them Behave, King George?* (1982); *Shh! We're Writing the Constitution* (1987).

November 19   Margaret W. Musgrove

Ashanti to Zulu: African Traditions (Dial, 1976)—1977 Caldecott Award winner.

November 21   Leo Politi

Song of the Swallows (Macmillan, 1981)—1950 Caldecott Award winner; *The Nicest Gift* (Scribner, 1973); *Three Stalks of Corn* (Macmillan, 1976); *Mr. Fong's Toy Shop* (Macmillan, 1978).

November 23   Marc Simont

Illustrator of many titles, including: Nate the Great series by Sharmat; *Volcanoes* by Branley; *If You Listen* by Zolotow; *No More Monsters for Me* by Parish.

November 24   Carlo Collodi

The Adventures of Pinocchio: Tale of a Puppet (Lothrop, 1983); Troll Associates series for grades 2–5: *Pinocchio and the Great Whale, Pinocchio Goes to School, Pinocchio and the Puppet Show, Pinocchio Meets the Cat and Fox.*

November 24   Mordicai Gerstein

Arnold of the Ducks (Harper, 1983); *Follow Me!* (Morrow, 1983); *Prince Sparrow* (Macmillan, 1984); *Roll Over!* (Crown, 1984); *The Room* (Harper, 1984); *William, Where Are You?* (Crown, 1985); *The Seal Mother* (Dial, 1986); *Tales of Pan* (Harper, 1986); *Mountains of Tibet* (Harper, 1987).

November 25   Marc Brown

Pickle Things (Parents, 1980); *The True Francine* (Avon, 1982); Arthur series published by Little, Brown: *Arthur Goes to Camp, Arthur's April Fool, Arthur's Christmas, Arthur's Eyes, Arthur's Halloween, Arthur's Nose, Arthur's Thanksgiving, Arthur's Tooth, Arthur's Valentine.*

November 26   Charles Schulz

The creator of the well-loved Peanuts gang. There are innumerable titles from which to select.

November 28   Stephanie Calmenson

Never Take a Pig to Lunch (Doubleday, 1982); *The Birthday Hat* (Putnam, 1983); *Where Is Grandma Potamus?* (Putnam, 1983); *The After-School Book* (Putnam, 1984); *All Aboard the Goodnight Train* (Putnam, 1984); *Waggleby of Fraggle Rock* (Holt, 1985); *The Shaggy Little Monster* (Simon & Schuster, 1986); *The Little Bunny* (Simon & Schuster, 1987); *The Little Chick* (Simon & Schuster, 1987).

November 28   Tomi Ungerer

The Beast of Monsieur Racine (Farrar, 1971); *Three Robbers* (Macmillan, 1975); *Crictor* (Harper, 1984); *Moon Man* (Harper, 1984).

November 30   Margot Zemach

Illustrator of *The Judge* (Farrar, 1969)—1970 Caldecott Honor book; *A Penny a Look* (Farrar, 1971); *Duffy and the Devil* (Farrar, 1986)—1974 Caldecott Award winner; *Mommy, Buy Me a China Doll* (Farrar, 1975); *It Could Always Be Worse* (Farrar, 1977)—1978 Caldecott Honor book; *The Three Wishes* (Farrar, 1986).

DECEMBER

December 5	Harve Zemach, *The Judge: An Untrue Tale* (drawing activity)
December 8	James Thurber, *Many Moons* (fill in)
December 9	Jean DeBrunhoff, *Babar and Father Christmas* (drawing activity)
December 10	Melvil Dewey, "Dewey's Favorite Nonfiction" (book list)
December 12	Barbara Emberley, *Drummer Hoff* (ABC order)
December 13	Leonard Weisgard, *The Little Island* (fill in)
December 14	Lorna Balian, *Bah! Humbug?* (writing activity)
December 16	Marie Hall Ets, *Nine Days to Christmas* (fill in)
December 16	Quentin Blake, *Mrs. Armitage on Wheels* (fill in)
December 19	Eve Bunting, *The Mother's Day Mice* (song writing)
December 20	Michael Berenstain, *Peat Moss & Ivy and the Birthday Present* (birthday listing)
December 24	John Langstaff, *Frog Went A-Courtin'* (rhyming words)
December 26	Jean Van Leeuwen, *Oliver, Amanda, and Grandmother Pig* (word meanings)
December 27	Ingri Parin D'Aulaire, *Abraham Lincoln* (true/false)
December 30	Mercer Mayer, *There's a Nightmare in My Closet* and *There's an Alligator Under My Bed* (writing comparison activity)

December Bookmarks
December Answer Key
December Authors Bibliography

DECEMBER AUTHORS

DATE	NAME	AUTHOR	ILLUSTRATOR	K	1	2	3
2	David Macaulay	X	X			X	X
5	Phyllis Adams	X			X	X	X
5	Harve Zemach	X	X			X	X
7	Ellen Weiss	X			X	X	X
8	Kin Platt	X				X	X
8	Padraic Colum	X					X
8	Edwin Tunis	X					X
8	James Thurber	X				X	X
9	Joel Chandler Harris	X				X	X
9	Jean DeBrunhoff	X	X	X	X	X	
9	Adelaide Holl	X		X	X	X	X
10	Melvil Dewey	Greatest Librarian of all times.					
12	Barbara Emberley	X				X	X
13	Leonard Weisgard		X				
14	Lorna Balian	X	X	X	X	X	
16	Marie Hall Ets	X		X	X	X	
16	Quentin Blake	X	X			X	X
16	Jane Belk Moncure	X			X	X	
17	David Kherdian	X				X	X
17	William Lipkind	X			X	X	
19	Eve Bunting	X				X	X
21	Michael Berenstain	X	X	X	X	X	
24	John Langstaff	X				X	X
25	Eth Clifford	X					X
26	Jean Van Leeuwen	X			X	X	
27	Ingri Parin D'Aulaire	X	X			X	X
29	E.W. Hildick	X					X
30	Mercer Mayer	X	X	X	X	X	X

HARVE ZEMACH

"The Judge: An Untrue Tale"

Read "The Judge: An Untrue Tale." Five people tried to warn the judge that something horrid was coming. But he wouldn't listen. Maybe he would have believed them if he had seen a picture of the creature.

Below is a description of the monster from "The Judge." Draw a picture that fits the words. I hope the judge listens to you!

Its eyes are scary

Its tail is hairy

Its paws have claws

It snaps its jaws

It growls, it groans

It chews up stones

It spreads its wings

And does bad things

It belches flame

It has no name

I tell you, Judge, we all better pray!

Name _____   Date _____

JAMES THURBER

"Many Moons"

Read "Many Moons." When a princess wants the moon, she gets the moon. Use the words in the Word Bank to finish these sentences about the princess and her moon.

1. A _____ wanted the _____.

2. The chamberlain said the moon was molten _____.

3. The wizard said the moon was green _____.

4. The mathematician said the moon was _____.

5. The princess said the moon was made of _____.

6. The _____ worried about the princess seeing the real moon.

7. The chamberlain said give her dark _____.

8. The wizard said to hang black velvet _____.

9. The mathematician said _____ would keep the night bright.

10. The princess said the sky _____ a new moon.

```
WORD BANK
asbestos    cheese    copper    curtains    fireworks
glasses     gold      grew      king        moon        princess
```

Name_____   Date_____

JEAN DE BRUNHOFF

"Babar and Father Christmas"

Read "Babar and Father Christmas." Jean's story includes a map of Father Christmas' cave. If you had a cave to live in, what kind of rooms would you have? What would you do in them? Use the outline below to show your friends what your cave home contains. Label it!

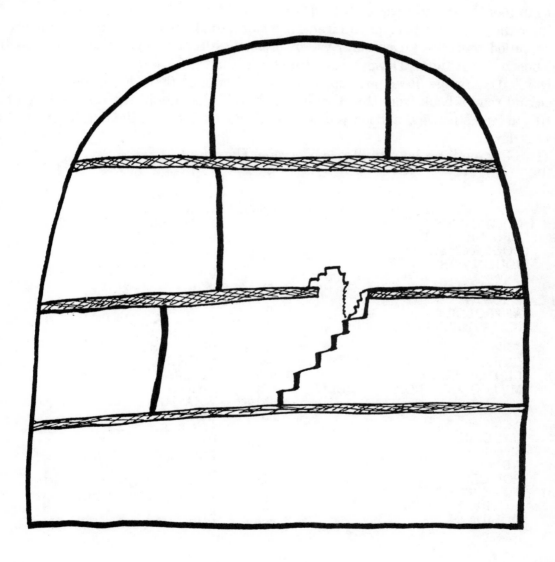

Name_____   Date_____

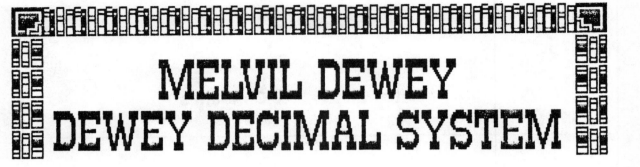

MELVIL DEWEY
DEWEY DECIMAL SYSTEM

December 10th is the birthday of Melvil Dewey. He created a way of organizing books that is used in America and all over the world. "Every book has a topic. Every topic has a number. That's how we shall find things," said Melvil. And we still do.

Over the years, millions of children have found the books they wanted by using the system called the Dewey Decimal System. Below are listed some of the favorites they have chosen. I call them "Dewey's Favorite Nonfiction."

Here's a challenge. Read one book from each grouping (000's, 100's, 200's, etc.). Select a topic and read a book from that Dewey number. Underline all the numbers you have read. If you find a nonfiction book you want to read that is not on the list, insert it in the correct order.

There's something here to please everyone. Have fun!

000s
001.64 COMPUTERS
001.9   UFO, BIGFOOT, ETC.
028.7   BOOKS OF FACTS
070   JOURNALISM

100s
133.1   GHOSTS
133.5   ASTROLOGY
152   BEHAVIOR, FEELINGS

200s
220   BIBLE
232.9   LIFE OF JESUS
292   MYTHOLOGY, ROMAN GREEK

300s
317.3   ALMANACS
331.7   CAREERS
332.4   MONEY
355.3   ARMY
363   POLICE
385-87 TRANSPORTATION
389   METRIC SYSTEM
394.2   HOLIDAYS

395   MANNERS
398.2   LEGENDS, FAIRY TALES
        FOLK TALES

400s
423   DICTIONARY, THESAURUS
468   SPANISH BOOKS

500s
507   SCIENCE EXPERIMENTS
510   NUMBERS
523.4   PLANETS
534   SOUND
541   CHEMISTRY, MATTER
551   EARTH
551.63 WEATHER FORECASTING
552   ROCKS
560   FOSSILS
567.9   DINOSAURS
573.3   PREHISTORIC MAN
574   ENVIRONMENTS
580   PLANTS, TREES, FLOWERS
591.5   ANIMAL BEHAVIOR
597   FISH
598.1   REPTILES, SNAKES

Name_____   Date_____

598.2	BIRDS		796.4	GYMNASTICS
599.1-.9	ANIMALS OF ALL KINDS		796.54	CAMPING
593	AMOEBA		796.6	BICYCLES
594	SEA SHELLS		796.7	AUTO RACING
595	INSECTS		796.8	BOXING, KARATE, JUDO
			796.9	ICE SKATING, HOCKEY, SKIING
600s			797.2	SWIMMING, SCUBA
600	INVENTIONS		798.2	HORSE RIDING
610*s*	MEDICINE		799.1	FISHING
612	BIOLOGY (MAN)		799.2	HUNTING
613.7	FITNESS		799.32	ARCHERY
613.8	DRUG ABUSE			
614	FIRST AID		*800s*	
625	MODELS, AIRPLANE, ETC.		808.8	STORY COLLECTIONS
627	UNDERSEA EXPLORATION		811	AMERICAN POETRY
629.133	AIRPLANES		812	DRAMA (PLAYS)
629.2	AUTOS, MOTORCYCLES		817	HUMOROUS COLLECTIONS
629.45	MANNED SPACE FLIGHT		821	ENGLISH POETRY
630	FARMING			
636.1-8	PETS, ALL KINDS		*900s*	
641.5	COOKING		904	WORLD HISTORY
683	WEAPONS		910.4	ACCOUNTS OF TRAVEL
			912	MAPS
700s			914-919	GEOGRAPHY OF VARIOUS COUNTRIES
704	ART TOPICS		917.3	GEOGRAPHY OF USA
720	ARCHITECTURE		920	COLLECTIVE BIOGRAPHIES
730	SCULPTURE		929.4	NAMES
736	ORIGAMI		929.6	HERALDRY
741	DRAWING		929.9	FLAGS
741.59	COMICS		930	HISTORY OF ANCIENT EGYPT, ROME, GREECE, ETC.
745.5	CRAFTS THINGS TO MAKE			
750	PAINTING			
769.56	POSTAGE STAMP COLLECTING		940	HISTORY OF EUROPE
778	PHOTOGRAPHY		940.3	WORLD WAR I
780	MUSIC		940.54	WORLD WAR II
791.4	TELEVISION, MOVIES		950	ASIA, CHINA, JAPAN, KOREA, ETC.
791.5	PUPPETS			
792	BALLET		960	AFRICA
793.7	PUZZLES, GAMES, RIDDLES		970	NORTH AMERICA
793.8	MAGIC		972	MEXICO
794.6	BOWLING		973.1-.9	U.S. HISTORY
796	SPORTS!!		977.3	ILLINOIS HISTORY
796.32	BASKETBALL, VOLLEYBALL		978.02	COWBOYS OF THE OLD WEST
796.332	FOOTBALL		980	SOUTH AMERICA
796.334	SOCCER		998	ARCTIC REGIONS AND ANTARCTICA
796.34	TENNIS			
796.357	BASEBALL		999	EXTRATERRESTRIAL WORLDS

Name _____   **Date** _____

BARBARA EMBERLEY

"Drummer Hoff"

Read "Drummer Hoff." Put the words in the Word Bank in alphabetical order.

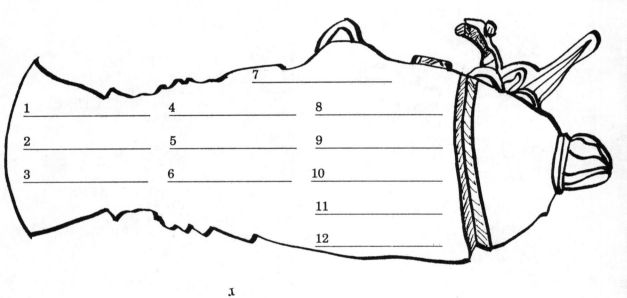

1 _____

2 _____

3 _____

4 _____

5 _____

6 _____

7 _____

8 _____

9 _____

10 _____

11 _____

12 _____

Illustration from *Drummer Hoff* adapted by Barbara Emberley, illustrated by Ed Emberley © 1967. Used by permission of the publisher, Prentice Hall, Inc., Englewood Cliffs, NJ.

WORD BANK					
drummer	carriage	corporal	private	barrel	fire
power	sergeant	rammer	shot	general	order

Name _____   Date _____

© 1989 by The Center for Applied Research in Education

LEONARD WEISGARD

"The Little Island"

Read "The Little Island." The story was written by Margaret Wise Brown under the pen name of Golden MacDonald. The illustrator Leonard Weisgard won the Caldecott Award. Use the words in the Word Bank to finish these sentences.

1. There was a little _____ in the _____.

2. Morning was _____ on the island.

3. One pear tree _____ on the island.

4. _____ crawled in from the sea to shed their _____.

5. Seals took care of their _____.

6. _____ built nests.

7. Gulls laid _____ on rocky _____.

8. A little _____ came to the island with some people.

9. He thought he was a _____ island in the air.

10. He didn't know all land is one land under the _____.

11. Autumn came and the ripe pears fell to the _____.

12. It's good to be a little island _____ by bright blue sea.

WORD BANK

babies	bloomed	eggs	fur		ground	island
kingfishers	kitten	ledges	lobsters	ocean	quiet	
sea	shells	surrounded				

Name_____ **Date**_____

LORNA BALIAN

"Bah! Humbug?"

Read "Bah! Humbug?" Margie knows there is a Santa Claus. And so do we. Write a short story about the night you met Santa Claus. Use the questions below to help you think about the plot (what events will happen) of your story.

1. In what room will you see Santa?

2. Will he have the special present you wanted this year?

3. What will you say if he forgot your special present? What if an elf sat on it? Or what if a reindeer stepped on it?

4. If Santa is cold and hungry, what will you give him?

5. What if he can't fit down the chimney of your next-door neighbor?

6. What if he happens to fall asleep next to your tree because he's tired?

7. What if he gives you the presents of your worst enemy by mistake? And your enemy has your presents? What will you do if your enemy doesn't want to give them back to you?

Now it's your turn to write "The Night Santa Crashed at My Place" or something. Write your story on the back of this page. Have fun!

© 1989 by The Center for Applied Research in Education

Name_____ **Date**_____

MARIE HALL ETS

"Nine Days to Christmas"

Read "Nine Days to Christmas: A Story of Mexico." Christmas is different in many countries. Use the words in the Word Bank to help you finish these sentences.

1. Ceci was excited about her first _____, a special Christmas party.

2. She knew there would be a _____, a special paper decoration.

3. Ceci saw old women on the street selling _____, corn-flour pancakes.

4. Ceci loved her doll, _____.

5. A big cat scared her _____.

6. Ceci's mother took her to the _____ to pick out her own piñata.

7. She picked the gold _____.

8. Ceci filled the piñata with oranges, lemons, _____, and _____.

9. Ceci did not want anyone to _____ the star.

10. When the piñata star broke, the star became _____.

WORD BANK

birds	candy	Gabina	hit	market	peanuts
piñata	posada	real	star	tortillas	

Name_____ Date_____

© 1989 by The Center for Applied Research in Education

QUENTIN BLAKE

"Mrs. Armitage on Wheels"

Read "Mrs. Armitage on Wheels." Use the words in the Word Bank to finish these sentences about a sweet lady who gets carried away with making her bicycle a better place to be.

1. Her bell was too soft, so she bought 3 _____.

2. Her chain made her hands dirty so she added a _____ of water and _____.

3. She also added a _____ kit with _____.

4. In case of hunger, she added a _____ for fruit and a holder for a _____ of lemonade.

5. She added a _____ for Breakspear.

6. For rainy days, she added two _____.

7. For cheerful music, she added a _____ and a mouth _____ so she could play along.

8. But when she added the _____, she crashed.

9. She started over with a pair of _____ _____.

10. But, she thought they _____ something.

WORD BANK

bottle	bucket	horns	needed	organ	radio	roller
sails	seat	skates	soap	tool	tray	umbrellas
wrenches						

Name _____   Date _____

© 1989 by The Center for Applied Research in Education

EVE BUNTING

Let's Write a New Song!

Not everyone can write music, but we can write words. Little Mouse made new words for the song, "Twinkle, Twinkle Little Star." He changed the words, but they still fit the rhythm of the song. Below are the words Little Mouse used. Can you change his words to make a Mother's Day song for your mom, or grandma, or aunt, or special lady you love? SURE YOU CAN!!

> We have brought a song to say,
> Happy, happy Mother's Day.
> No one's mother is so nice,
> Love from all your little mice.

From *The Mother's Day Mice* by Eve Bunting, illustrated by Jan Brett. Text copyright © 1986 by Eve Bunting. Reprinted by permission of Clarion Books/Ticknor & Fields, a Houghton Mifflin Company.

Here's an example:

My sweet present has no bow,
For the one that I love so.
Hope your day is oh so fine,
Hope you like this song of mine!

Count the syllables in "Twinkle, Twinkle Little Star." That will help you keep the correct rhythm. The example also has 7 syllables or BEATS per line.

Line 1   seven: Twinkle, twinkle little star
Line 2   seven: How I wonder what you are.
Line 3   seven: Up above the world so high
Line 4   seven: Like a diamond in the sky.

You can add two more lines, if you want.

NOW IT'S YOUR TURN:

_____

_____

Name_____   Date_____

MICHAEL BERENSTAIN

"Peat Moss & Ivy and the Birthday Present"

Read "Peat Moss & Ivy and the Birthday Present." Everyone has a birthday, even authors. Select one of the authors from December and send him or her a birthday card that you made all by yourself. Make sure you explain which book you liked best. What a surprise!

December 2 David Macaulay
c/o Houghton Mifflin
Two Park Street
Boston MA 02108

December 14 Lorna Balian
c/o Abingdon Press
201 Eighth Avenue South, Box 801
Nashville, TN 37202

December 19 Eve Bunting
c/o Clarion Books
52 Vanderbilt Avenue
New York, NY 10017

December 21 Michael Berenstain
c/o Random House Publishers, Inc.
201 East 50th Street
New York, NY 10022

Decmber 26 Jean Van Leeuwen
c/o Dial Books for Young Readers
Two Park Avenue
New York, NY 10016

December 30 Mercer Mayer
c/o Dial Books for Young Readers
Two Park Avenue
New York, NY 10016

Name_____ Date_____

JOHN LANGSTAFF

"Frog Went A-Courtin'"

Read "Frog Went A-Courtin'." This "song" story has a lively bounce as the guests arrive with their presents. Fill in the blanks with the correct rhyming word.

1. Little white moth brought the _____.

2. Old black bug brought the cider _____.

3. The raccoon brought a silver _____.

4. Mr. Snake brought the _____.

5. The bumblebee brought a banjo on his _____.

6. Gray goose brought a fiddle to cut _____.

7. Ants love to _____.

8. Fly ate all the wedding _____.

9. Little Chick ate herself _____.

10. But the old mean cat put a stop to _____.

11. Frog and mouse took their romance to _____.

WORD BANK					
cake	dance	France	jug	knee	loose
pie	sick	spoon	tablecloth		that

Name_____ **Date**_____

JEAN VAN LEEUWEN

"Oliver, Amanda, and Grandmother Pig"

Read "Oliver, Amanda, and Grandmother Pig." Use the words from the Word Bank to match the words with their meanings.

1. — — — — —   things to read

2. — — — —   seven days

3. — — — — — — — —   traveling bag

4. — — —   short sleep

5. — — — — —   argue

6. — — —   make tears

7. — — — —   letters and stuff

8. — — — — — —   night meal

9. — — — — —   stay awhile

10. — — — — —   no noise

WORD BANK

books	cry	dinner	fight	mail
nap	quiet	suitcase	visit	week

Name_____ **Date**_____

INGRI PARIN D'AULAIRE

"Abraham Lincoln"

Read "Abraham Lincoln." This book by Ingri and her husband Edgar is filled with facts about Abraham Lincoln. Place a T in front of the TRUE sentences. Place an F in front of the FALSE statements. Circle the word or words in the FALSE statements that make them FALSE.

1. ___ Abe was born in a brick home.

2. ___ Abe learned to read and write when he was six.

3. ___ Abe loved to hunt deer.

4. ___ Abe's mother died when he was young.

5. ___ Abe's new mother was lazy.

6. ___ Abe wrote with paper and pencil by candlelight.

7. ___ Abe thought slavery was a good idea.

8. ___ Abe left home when he was 21 to try his luck with the world.

9. ___ Abe joined the army to fight Black Hawk, an Illinois Indian chief.

10. ___ Abe opened a store and studied to become a doctor.

11. ___ Abe was elected to serve in Springfield, the capitol of Illinois.

12. ___ Abe married Mary Dott.

13. ___ Abe had three sons with Mary.

14. ___ Abe liked to make speeches.

15. ___ Abe was elected senator before Judge Douglas.

16. ___ Abe ran for president and lost by a few votes.

17. ___ Abe said the slaves had to stay slaves forever.

18. ___ Abe made the South pay all the bills for the war.

19. ___ Everybody loved Abe.

Name _____   **Date** _____

MERCER MAYER

"There's a Nightmare in My Closet"
"There's an Alligator Under My Bed"

_____

Read "There's a Nightmare in My Closet" and "There's an Alligator Under My Bed." Mercer wrote the nightmare book in 1968 and the alligator book in 1987. We know his pictures are always great. But how are the stories the same and different? Answer these questions about the stories.

1. What keeps the little boy awake:

Nightmare story: _____

Alligator story: _____

2. Where does the thing live?

Nightmare story _____

Alligator story _____

3. What does the little boy do to the thing?

Nightmare story _____

_____

Alligator story _____

_____

4. Is the nightmare happy at the end of the story? Why or why not?

_____

_____

5. On the back of this page, describe how dad will get into his car in the morning. Will the little boy help? How would you get an alligator out of your garage without hurting it?

Name_____   **Date**_____

DECEMBER
READERS!

DECEMBER

DECEMBER

DECEMBER

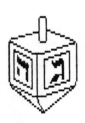
DECEMBER
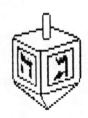

DECEMBER ANSWER KEY

JAMES THURBER: *Many Moons*

1. princess; moon
2. copper
3. cheese
4. asbestos
5. gold
6. king
7. glasses
8. curtains
9. fireworks
10. grew

BARBARA EMBERLEY: *Drummer Hoff*

1. barrel
2. carriage
3. corporal
4. drummer
5. fire
6. general
7. order
8. powder
9. private
10. rammer
11. sergeant
12. shot

LEONARD WEISGARD: *The Little Island*

1. island; ocean
2. quiet
3. bloomed
4. lobsters; shells
5. babies
6. kingfishers
7. eggs; ledges
8. cat
9. fur
10. sea
11. ground
12. surrounded

MARIE HALL ETS: *Nine Days to Christmas*

1. posada
2. piñata
3. tortillas
4. Gabina
5. birds
6. market
7. star
8. candy; peanuts
9. hit
10. real

QUENTIN BLAKE: *Mrs. Armitage on Wheels*

1. horns
2. bucket; soap
3. tool; wrenches
4. tray; bottle
5. seat
6. umbrellas
7. radio; organ
8. sails
9. roller skates
10. needed

JOHN LANGSTAFF: *Frog Went A-Courtin'*

1. tablecloth
2. jug
3. spoon
4. cake
5. knee
6. loose
7. dance
8. pie
9. sick
10. that
11. France

December Answer Key

JEAN VAN LEEUWEN: *Oliver, Amanda, and Grandmother Pig*

1. books
2. week
3. suitcase
4. nap
5. fight
6. cry
7. mail
8. dinner
9. visit
10. quiet

INGRI PARIN D'AULAIRE: *Abraham Lincoln*

1. F (brick)
2. T
3. F (loved)
4. T
5. F (lazy)
6. F (paper and pencil)
7. F (good)
8. T
9. T
10. F (doctor)
11. F (was elected)
12. F (Dott)
13. T
14. T
15. F (before)
16. F (lost)
17. F (stay slaves forever)
18. F (pay)
19. T

MERCER MAYER: *There's a Nightmare in My Closet* and *There's an Alligator Under My Bed*

1. a nightmare; an alligator
2. in the closet; under the bed
3. invites him to sleep in his bed; tricks him into the garage
4. yes, because he has a friend to sleep with
5. Answers will vary

DECEMBER AUTHORS BIBLIOGRAPHY

December 2   David Macaulay

Cathedral (Houghton Mifflin, 1973)—1974 Caldecott Honor book; *Castle* (Houghton Mifflin, 1977)—1978 Caldecott Honor book.

December 5   Phyllis Adams

Excellent first grade titles distributed by Caroline House for Modern Curriculum Press, under Pippin easy-to-read series: *Pippin at the Gym, Pippin Cleans Up, Pippin Eats Out, Pippin Goes to Work, Pippin Learns a Lot, Pippin's Lucky Penny*; Troll family series: *A Dog Is Not a Troll, A Troll, a Truck & a Cookie, Go, Wendall, Go, Hi Dog*; Cora Cow series.

December 5   Harve Zemach

The Judge: An Untrue Tale (Farrar, 1969)—1970 Caldecott Honor book; *A Penny a Look : An Old Story* (Farrar, 1971); *Duffy and the Devil* (Farrar, 1986)—1974 Caldecott Award winner; illustrator of *Mommy, Buy Me a China Doll* (Farrar, 1975); *Princess & Froggie* (Farrar, 1975).

December 7   Ellen Weiss

Millicent Maybe (Avon, 1980); *Mokey's Birthday Present* (Holt, 1985); *Pirates of Tarnoonga* (Random, 1986); *Telephone Time* (Random, 1986); *The Maxxe Steele Trap: A Robo Force Adventure* (Random, 1987).

December 8   Kin Platt

Big Max (Harper, 1978); *Big Max in the Mystery of the Missing Moose* (Harper, 1985).

December 8   Padraic Colum

The Golden Fleece (Macmillan, 1983); *The Children of Odin: A Book of Northern Myths* (Macmillan, 1984).

December 8   Edwin Tunis

These are excellent resources with pictures of the time. Although the reading level will be too high, children can learn from looking: *Colonial Living* (Harper, 1976); *Frontier Living* (Harper, 1976).

December 8   James Thurber

Many Moons (HBJ, 1943)—1944 Caldecott Award winner; *The Great Quillow* (HBJ, 1975); *Thurber Carnival* (Harper, 1975); *Night the Ghost Got In* (Creative Education, 1983).

December Authors Bibliography

December 9   Joel Chandler Harris

Uncle Remus (Penguin, 1982).

December 9   Jean de Brunhoff

The Babar books are published by Random House: *Babar & Father Christmas, Babar & His Children, Babar & Zephir, Babar the King, Meet Babar & His Family, The Story of Babar, Travels of Babar.*

December 9   Adelaide Holl

Rain Puddle (Lothrop, 1965); *Remarkable Egg* (Lothrop, 1968); Small Bear series published by Garrard: *Bedtime for Bears, Small Bear & the Secret Surprise, Small Bear Builds a Playhouse, Small Bear Solves a Mystery, Small Bear's Birthday Party, Small Bear's Busy Day, Small Bear's Name Hunt, Wake Up, Small Bear.*

December 10   Melvil Dewey

Dewey Decimal Classification System: three Volumes Index, Schedules, Tables—now in 19th edition.

December 12   Barbara Emberley

Drummer Hoff (Prentice Hall, 1967)—1968 Caldecott Award winner.

December 13   Leonard Weisgard

Illustrator of *The Little Island* (Doubleday, 1946)—1947 Caldecott Award winner; illustrator of other Margaret Wise Brown books: *Quiet Noisy Book* (Harper, 1950), *Indoor Noisy Book* (Harper, 1962); *Baby Elephant & the Secret Wishes* with Sesyle Joslin (HBJ, 1962).

December 14   Lorna Balian

Author/Illustrator of these books, all published by Abingdon: *Amelia's Nine Lives, The Aminal, Bah! Humbug?, Humbug Rabbit, Leprechauns Never Lie, Mother's Mother's Day, Sometimes It's Turkey, Sometimes It's Feathers, The Sweet Touch, A Sweetheart for Valentine.*

December 16   Marie Hall Ets

In the Forest (Viking, 1944)—1945 Caldecott Honor book; *Play With Me* (Viking, 1955)—1956 Caldecott Honor book; *Nine Days to Christmas* (Viking, 1959)—1960 Caldecott Award winner; *Elephant in a Well* (Viking, 1972); *Just Me* (Penguin, 1978).

December 16   Quentin Blake

Illustrated most titles written by Roald Dahl; his own titles include: *Quentin Blake's Nursery Rhyme Book* (Harper, 1984); *The Story of the Dancing Frog* (Knopf, 1985); *Mrs. Armitage on Wheels (Knopf, 1988).*

December Authors Bibliography

December 16   Jane Belk Moncure

Has written over 240 titles for preschool and early elementary children. Has written series about the consonants, vowels, feelings, holidays, religion, seasons, and beginning-to-read books, most notably the Word Bird series available from Child's World: *Word Bird Builds a City, Word Bird Makes Words with Cat, Word Bird Makes Words with Dog.*

December 17   David Kherdian

Mystery of the Diamond in the Wood (Knopf, 1983); several titles illustrated by his wife Nonny Hogrogian: *Poems Here and Now* (Greenwillow, 1976), *Right Now* (Knopf, 1983), *The Animal* (Knopf, 1984).

December 17   William Lipkind

Finder Keepers, illustrated by Nicolas Mordvinoff (HBJ, 1973)—1952 Caldecott Award winner.

December 19   Eve Bunting

These are third grade titles: *Day of the Dinosaur* (EMC, 1975), *Death of a Dinosaur* (EMC, 1975), *Dinosaur Trap* (EMC, 1975), *Escape from Tyrannosaurus* (EMC, 1975). Her children's picture books include: *St. Patrick's Day in the Morning* (Clarion, 1980); *Scary, Scary Halloween* (Clarion, 1986); *Mother's Day Mice* (Clarion, 1986)—this probably should have been the 1987 Caldecott winner!; the Skate Patrol trilogy: published by Whitman: *The Skate Patrol, The Skate Patrol Rides Again, The Skate Patrol and the Mystery Writer.*

December 21   Michael Berenstain

He is the son of Stan and Jan Berenstain (Bears): *The Troll Book* (Random, 1980); *Sorcerer's Scrapbook* (Random, 1981); *Creature Catalog: A Monster Watcher's Guide* (Random, 1982); *Peat Moss & Ivy and the Birthday Present* (Random, 1986); *Peat Moss and Ivy's Backyard Adventure* (Random, 1986).

December 24   John Langstaff

Frog Went A-Courtin' (HBJ, 1955)—1956 Caldecott Award winner; *Over in the Meadow* (HBJ, 1967); *Oh, A-Hunting We Will Go* (Macmillan, 1974).

December 25   Eth Clifford

Help! I'm a Prisoner in the Library (Houghton Mifflin, 1979 or Scholastic, 1985); *Killer Swan* (Houghton Mifflin, 1980); *Dastardly Murder of Dirty Pete* (Houghton Mifflin, 1981); *Just Tell Me When We're Dead* (Hougton Mifflin, 1983, or Scholastic, 1985); *Harvey's Horrible Snake Disaster* (Houghton Mifflin, 1984); *I Never Wanted to Be Famous* (Houghton Mifflin, 1985).

December 26   Jean Van Leeuwen

More Tales of Amanda Pig (Dial, 1981); *More Tales of Oliver Pig* (Dial, 1981); *Amanda Pig & Her Big Brother* (Dial, 1982); *Tales of Amanda Pig* (Dial, 1983).

December 27   Ingri Parin D'Aulaire

Wife of Edgar Parin D'Aulaire, also an author/illustrator. See "September" for complete list of their books.

December 29   E. W. Hildick

These mysteries for grades 3–6 are published by Macmillan: *Case of the Felon's Fiddle, Case of the Four Flying Fingers, Case of the Muttering Mummy, Case of the Phantom Frog, Case of the Secret Scribbler, Case of the Slingshot Sniper, Secret of the Snowbound Spy*; mysteries for grades 3–6 published by Archway: *Case of the Bashful Bank Robber, Case of the Condemned Cat, Case of the Invisible Dog, Case of the Nervous Newsboy*; Ghost Squad series: *Ghost Squad & the Halloween Conspiracy* (Dutton, 1985), *Ghost Squad Flies* (Dutton, 1985), *Ghost Squad Breaks Through* (Warner, 1986).

December 30   Mercer Mayer

He has an impressive list of books, from wordless picture books to exquisitely illustrated award winners. Wordless picture books published by Dial: *A Boy, A Dog & A Frog, Frog on His Own, Frog Goes to Dinner, Frog, Where Are You?, Ah-Choo, Hiccup, and Oops*; Little Critter series published by Western: *Bedtime Book, Counting Book, Just Me & My Dad, Just Me & My Little Sister*; for second grade readers: *What Do You Do with a Kangaroo?* (Scholastic, 1975); *There's a Nightmare in My Closet* (Dial, 1976); *You're the Scaredy Cat* (Macmillan, 1980); *Terrible Troll* (Dial, 1981); *Whinnie the Lovesick Dragon* (Macmillan, 1986); *There's an Alligator Under My Bed* (Dial, 1987).

JANUARY

January 3   Carolyn Haywood, *A Valentine Fantasy* (sending valentines)

January 4   Jacob Grimm, *The Devil with the Three Golden Hairs*, illustrated by Nonny Hogrogian (fill in)

January 4   Beverly Fiday, *Patience: Our Own Story* (classroom book)

January 6   Carl Sandburg, Write a Poem
Carl Sandburg Write a Poem II

January 7   Kay Chorao, *Lester's Overnight* (idioms)

January 10   Remy Charlip, *Fortunately* (writing activity)

January 18   Raymond Briggs, *The Snowman* (dialogue writing activity)

January 18   A. A. Milne, Write a Poem I
A. A. Milne, Write a Poem II

January 18   Arthur Ransome, *The Fool of the World and His Flying Ship* (designing a ship)

January 22   Blair Lent, *The Funny Little Woman* (fill in)

January 27   Harry Allard, *Miss Nelson Is Missing* (fill in)

January 29   Bill Peet, *Big Bad Bruce* (fill in)

January 29   Rosemary Wells, *Noisy Nora* (poem fill in)

January 31   Gerald McDermott, *Arrow to the Sun* (Indian drawing activity)

    January Bookmarks
    January Answer Key
    January Authors Bibliography

JANUARY AUTHORS

DATE	NAME	AUTHOR/ILLUSTRATOR		READING LEVEL			
				K	1	2	3
1	Barbara Williams	X		X	X	X	
2	Isaac Asimov	X					X
2	Crosby Bonsall	X		X	X	X	
3	Joan Walsh Anglund	X	X	X	X	X	
3	Carolyn Haywood	X			X	X	
4	Beverly Fiday	X		X	X	X	
4	Jacob Grimm	X				X	X
4	Fernando Krahn	X	X	X	X	X	X
6	Carl Sandburg	X				X	X
7	Kay Chorao	X	X	X	X	X	
7	Eleanor Clymer	X					X
8	Lee J. Ames		X			X	X
9	Clyde Robert Bulla	X					X
10	Remy Charlip	X			X	X	
12	Clement Hurd		X				
12	Charles Perrault	X				X	X
13	N.M. Bodecker	X			X	X	
15	William Arden	X					X
17	John Bellairs	X					X
18	Raymond Briggs	X	X	X	X	X	
18	A. A. Milne	X		X	X	X	X
18	Arthur Ransome	X				X	X
22	Margaret Hillert	X		X	X		
22	Blair Lent	X		X	X	X	X
22	Brian Wildsmith	X	X		X		
27	Lewis Carroll	X					X
27	Harry Allard	X		X	X	X	
29	Bill Peet	X				X	X
29	Rosemary Wells	X			X	X	
30	Tony Johnston	X		X	X	X	
31	Gerald McDermott	X	X			X	X

CAROLYN HAYWOOD

"A Valentine Fantasy"

Read "A Valentine Fantasy." Use the words in the Word Bank to finish these sentences about how the heart became a Valentine symbol.

1. Once there lived a boy named _____.

2. His uncle made things from _____.

3. The uncle made the boy a bow with _____, but the boy never shot any

   _____.

4. The king of the country fell in _____.

5. The future queen wanted the _____ of a golden bluebird.

6. They put Valentine in a _____ because he would not shoot the bird.

7. The dungeon was _____ and _____.

8. The bluebird brought Valentine a _____ heart.

9. The king took the heart to the princess in a red _____ box.

10. The king proclaimed a _____ day.

11. Hearts given in love are called _____.

12. Flocks of _____ came to the wedding.

WORD BANK

animals	arrows	bluebirds	cold	dark	dungeon
gold	golden	heart	love	special	Valentine
valentines	velvet				

Name_____ **Date**_____

JACOB GRIMM

"The Devil with the Three Golden Hairs"

Read "The Devil with the Three Golden Hairs." Use the words in the Word Bank to finish these sentences about the very lucky boy.

1. Once, a very _____ boy was born to a poor family.

2. He was to marry the king's _____.

3. The poor couple took _____ for their son.

4. The king put the boy in a _____ and threw it in the _____.

5. A _____ pulled him from the river.

6. By accident, the king _____ the boy.

7. He sent him with a _____ to the queen.

8. He stayed at a house that belonged to _____.

9. They read the letter and _____ the message.

10. The boy married the _____.

11. The boy had to pass a _____ to stay married.

12. He had to get three golden hairs from the _____.

13. The devil's _____ helped him.

WORD BANK

box	changed	daughter	devil	discovered	gold
grandmother	letter	lucky	miller	princess	river
test	thieves				

Name _____   Date _____

© 1989 by The Center for Applied Research in Education

BEVERLY FIDAY

"Patience: What Is It?"

Read "Patience: What Is It?" Everyone can use a little patience. Second and third graders need patience for different reasons than first graders.

On the next page, write a sentence that describes a time when you need patience.

Remember:

Every sentence starts with a capital letter.
Every sentence ends with a period (.) or exclamation point(!)
Print or write neatly.
You may use some of these examples to help you start.

I need patience to…
Patience is waiting to…
    waiting for…
It takes patience to…
It's hard to be patient when…

Draw a picture to go with your sentence.

Your teacher will staple all the pages together and make a classroom book. Ask if your class can have a COVER DESIGN CONTEST. The best picture goes on the front of the book. The second place winner goes on the back cover.

I CAN BE PATIENT!

Name_____ **Date**_____

BEVERLY FIDAY

"Patience: What Is It?"

_____

_____

_____

_____

_____

Name_____ **Date**_____

CARL SANDBURG

"Write a Poem"

Read "Paper I" by Carl Sandburg from his book called *Wind Song*. Now that you know what he thinks of paper, help me write a poem called "Friends" by filling in the blanks.

FRIENDS

by

US

Friend is three kinds: sitters, runners, and jumpers.

Some will sit when you want to _____.

Some will run when you want to _____.

Some will jump when you want to _____.

Some friends are sitters who love to jump _____.

Some friends are jumpers who sit on a porch and count _____ at night.

Some friends are runners who jump over _____ and sit under a tree by a cool,

blue _____.

Are you a sitter, a runner, or a jumper?

As for me—I'm all _____!

WORD BANK

bushes   jump   lake   rope   run   sit   stars   three

Name_____   **Date**_____

CARL SANDBURG

"Write a Poem II"

Read "Do You Want Affidavits?" by Carl Sandburg from *Early Moon*. Affidavits are sworn statements that something is true. They are used in trials. But in this poem Sandburg also mentions "wishing windows." Read his poem again and write about your wishing window—by yourself. I'll help you start. Remember: It doesn't need to rhyme, but it can IF YOU WANT IT THAT WAY!

Wishes from My Window

For rainbows in my soup, I'd wish

and lots of chocolate on my dish.

_____

_____

_____

_____

_____

_____

_____

_____

There are many more I could name—you bet!

But just tell me one thing—how many do I get?

Name _____ **Date** _____

KAY CHORAO

"Lester's Overnight"

Read "Lester's Overnight." Lester has a very wonderful imagination. It works well with the things he does not understand. He didn't know that sentences do not mean exactly what they say sometimes. When that happens, they are called idioms. Here is a list of the things Lester did not understand.

They are *tied up* with your father's employer.
Meet my new *tiger cat*
Put on your pajamas like a *good little lamb.*
Night (knight) is upon us.

Here is another list of idioms. Use the frames on the next page to draw silly pictures of what the idioms mean. Print the idiom under the picture.

Turn left at the next fork in the road.

Don't let the cat out of the bag.

Cat got your tongue?

He really put his foot in his mouth.

Don't rock the boat.

Stop pulling my leg.

Lend me a hand.

Go fly a kite.

It's raining cats and dogs.

He's in hot water now.

They were chewing the fat

and shooting the breeze.

Up the creek without a paddle.

He's a ball of fire.

Zip your lip.

Name_____   **Date**_____

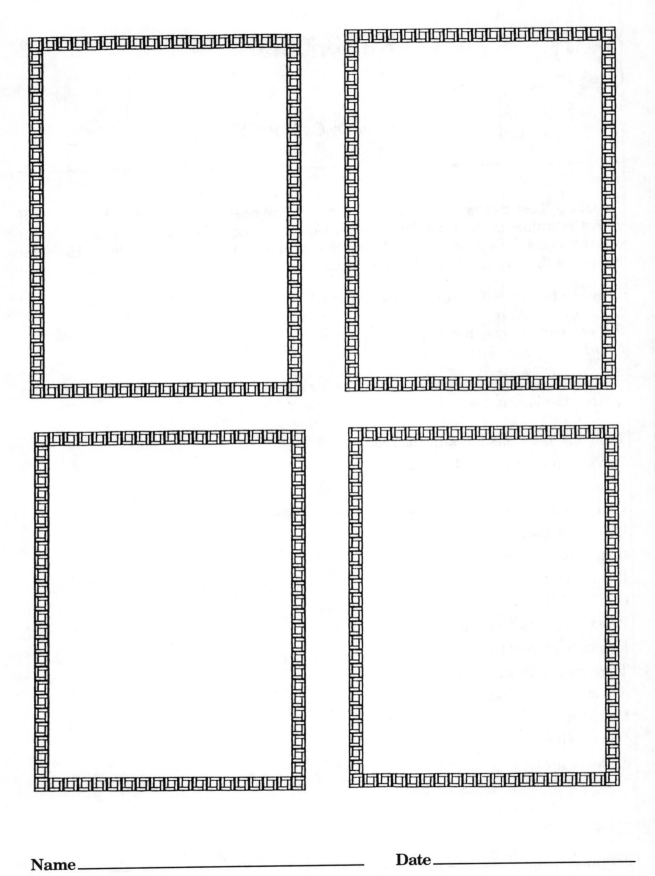

Name_____ **Date**_____

REMY CHARLIP

"Fortunately"

Read "Fortunately." Remy Charlip has quite an imagination. But you do too! Write a story like "Fortunately." Notice how Remy's story has many twists and turns. Just as the hero has a problem, something saves him. Read the example. Then write a story that has a fortunate ending.

One day just before Christmas vacation, I was late for school.

Fortunately, dad gave me a ride.

Unfortunately, his car broke down.

Fortunately, Santa was flying by on a test run.

Unfortunately, I fell out of the sleigh.

Fortunately, a condor flew by and saved me by the seat of my pants.

Unfortunately, my pants ripped.

Fortunately, I landed in a snowbank.

Unfortunately, the principal saw me come in late.

Fortunately, he was in the Christmas spirit.

Unfortunately, I still had a detention.

Fortunately, it snowed so hard everyone stayed.

Unfortunately, so did my principal.

Fortunately, he let us have a party!

Name _____ **Date** _____

RAYMOND BRIGGS

"The Snowman"

Look at the pictures in "The Snowman." This is still a beautiful story without words. You can make it your own story by writing a story to go with the pictures. You can write a story that is the dialog between you and a snowman.

Writing dialog means thinking about punctuation too. Everything a character says must be in QUOTATION marks (" "). Use the examples below to see where the commas and quotation marks go. Practice by inserting your dialog ideas into the form. Then write a complete story on a clean piece of paper.

"_____," I said.

"_____," said the snowman.

"_____," I said.

"_____," mumbled the snowman.

"_____," I asked.

"_____," said the snowman.

"_____," I said.

"_____," shouted the snowman.

"_____," I whispered.

"_____," said the snowman.

© 1989 by The Center for Applied Research in Education

Name_____   Date_____

A. A. MILNE

"Write a Poem I"

Read "Daffodowndilly" from *When We Were Very Young*. Milne wrote about a daffodil. Let's write about something scary! Practice by filling in these blanks. CLUE: The words that fill the blanks are rhyming words. Give the poem a name on the title line and the author line below.

Write a poem that describes something after you finish this.

_____
      title

He wears a scaly coat of _____.

His roar is decidely mean.

His wings are as black as night,

To children, he gives a terrible _____.

His teeth are blazing white,

Flames from his maul are brilliantly _____.

And he bellows for everyone to hear,

"Are there any hot dogs or marshmallows _____?"

"_____" by David Fiday and _____
                                   your name

Name_____   **Date**_____

A. A. MILNE

"Write a Poem II"

_____

Read "If I Were King" from *When We Were Very Young*. Finish these poems. Boys can be Kings. Girls can be Queens! You can make these poems longer by using another sheet of paper.

IF I WERE KING

I wish I were a King,

Then I could do anything.

If I were King of Spain,

I'd _____.

If I were King of France,

I _____.

I think if I were King of Greece,

I _____.

IF I WERE QUEEN

I wish I were a Queen,

I promise not to do anything mean.

If I were Queen of Spain,

I'd _____.

If I were Queen of France,

I _____.

I think if I were Queen of Greece,

I _____.

Name _____   Date _____

ARTHUR RANSOME

"The Fool of the World and the Flying Ship"

Read "The Fool of the World and the Flying Ship." The story was written by Arthur Ransome whose birthday is in January. The illustration won Uri Shulevitz a Caldecott Award. His birthday is in February.

The flying ship is a beautiful boat. If you had a flying ship, what would it look like? Draw your ship in the space below. Make Arthur and Uri proud of you!

Name _____ **Date** _____

BLAIR LENT

"The Funny Little Woman"

Read "The Funny Little Woman." Blair Lent won a Caldecott Award for his unusual pictures. He tells the story of the little old woman. When she leaves her house, we can still see what is happening there because Mr. Lent draws pictures of it too.

Use the words in the Word Bank to finish these sentences.

1. In _____ there lived a funny little woman.

2. She made _____ out of rice.

3. One day, one of them fell into a _____.

4. The wicked _____ lived down there.

5. The funny little woman was not _____ of the Oni.

6. The Oni wanted her to _____ for them.

7. They gave her a _____ paddle.

8. The funny little woman _____ her little house.

9. Oni do not swim, so they _____ the river.

10. The funny little woman got stuck in the _____.

11. The Oni laughed so hard, the _____ came out of their mouths.

12. The funny little woman became the _____ woman in Japan. Tee hee hee!

WORD BANK

afraid	cook	drank	dumplings	hole	Japan
magic	missed	mud	Oni	richest	river

Name _____   **Date** _____

HARRY ALLARD

"Miss Nelson Is Missing"

Read "Miss Nelson is Missing." Use the words in the Word Bank to finish these sentences about Miss Nelson's nasty class and how they learn their lesson.

1. The kids were _____ in Miss Nelson's room.

2. They loved to throw _____.

3. Miss Nelson asked them to _____ down.

4. They were even _____ during _____ hour.

5. One day, Miss Viola _____ came to teach.

6. She acted like a real _____.

7. She gave them lots of _____.

8. They wanted to _____ Miss Nelson.

9. Maybe she was eaten by a _____.

10. Maybe she went to _____.

11. Was she carried off by a herd of angry _____?

12. In Miss Nelson's _____, there is a black _____ and a _____— in case she needs them again.

WORD BANK

butterflies	closet	dress	find	homework	Mars
misbehaving	rude	settle	shark	spitballs	story
substitute	swamp	wig	witch		

Name_____ Date_____

BILL PEET

"Big Bad Bruce"

Read "Big Bad Bruce." Bill wrote this story to show us that sometimes, things just don't change.

1. Big bad Bruce was a _____.

2. He rolled _____ down hills.

3. He liked to frighten other _____.

4. One of his boulders almost hit a _____.

5. She made him a very special _____.

6. After his nap, Big Bad Bruce was very _____.

7. Quail _____ him on his head.

8. Rabbits _____ him.

9. The witch's cat saved him from the _____.

10. Bruce ate out of the cat's _____.

11. The witch liked _____ animals.

12. Little bad Bruce rolled _____ at _____.

13. Some people or animals never _____.

© 1989 by The Center for Applied Research in Education

WORD BANK

animals	bear	beetles	boulders	bowl	chased
change	little	pebbles	pecked	pie	river
tiny	witch				

Name_____   **Date**_____

ROSEMARY WELLS

"Noisy Nora"

Read "Noisy Nora." Everyone needs a little love or a hug each day. Nora couldn't wait. But she did because she had a brother and a sister. Sometimes it is difficult to wait. Finish this poem about "I Need a Hug." THE CLUE IS THAT THE MISSING WORDS RHYME!

MAKE A POEM OF YOUR OWN ON THE LINES BELOW.

I NEED A HUG!

I need a hug, and I need it NOW.

If you don't hurry, I'll go find a _____.

I need a hug, I can hardly WAIT.

If you don't hurry, I'll go find a _____.

I need a hug, you're running out of TIME.

I'll even give you money, how about a _____?

I need a hug, don't you need one TOO?

If you hug me honey, I'll hug _____!

_____
title

_____

_____

_____

_____

_____

Name_____ **Date**_____

GERALD MCDERMOTT

"Arrow to the Sun"

Read "Arrow to the Sun." Gerald McDermott took an old Indian tale and gave it beautiful illustrations. He did such a good job he won the Caldecott Award.

Indian designs don't use many colors, but the black background really makes the colors look brighter. Notice the jagged lines and the patterns they use. Color the example. Then draw an Indian design of your own.

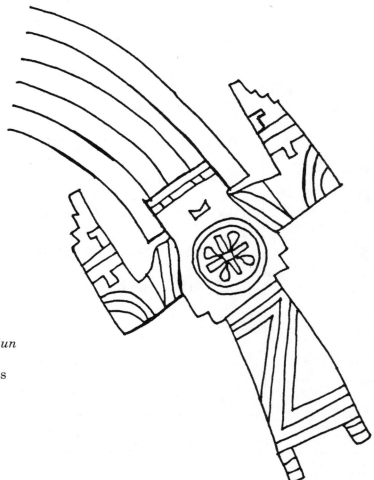

Illustration from *Arrow to the Sun* by Gerald McDermott. Copyright © 1974 by Gerald McDermott. All rights reserved. Reprinted by permission of Viking Penguin.

© 1989 by The Center for Applied Research in Education

Name_____   Date_____

 # JANUARY
READERS

 # LIVE THE DREAM,
READ!

 # JANUARY
WARM UP WITH A GOOD BOOK

 # SLIDE INTO A
GOOD BOOK!

 # OUR BOOKS WARM
THE COLDEST DAYS

JANUARY ANSWER KEY

CAROLYN HAYWOOD: *A Valentine Fantasy*

1. Valentine
2. gold
3. arrows; animals
4. love
5. heart
6. dungeon
7. cold; dark
8. golden
9. velvet
10. special
11. valentines
12. bluebirds

JACOB GRIMM: *The Devil with the Three Golden Hairs*

1. lucky
2. daughter
3. gold
4. box; river
5. miller
6. discovered
7. letter
8. thieves
9. changed
10. princess
11. test
12. devil
13. grandmother

CARL SANDBURG: *Write a Peom*

1. run
2. jump
3. sit
4. rope
5. stars
6. bushes
7. lake
8. three

BLAIR LENT: *The Funny Little Woman*

1. Japan
2. dumplings
3. hole
4. Oni
5. afraid
6. cook
7. magic
8. missed
9. drank
10. mud
11. river
12. richest

HENRY ALLARD: *Miss Nelson Is Missing*

1. misbehaving
2. spitballs
3. settle
4. rude; story
5. Swamp
6. witch
7. homework
8. find
9. shark
10. Mars
11. butterflies
12. closet; dress; wig

BILL PEET: *Big Bad Bruce*

1. bear
2. boulders
3. animals
4. witch
5. pie
6. tiny
7. pecked

8. chased
9. river
10. bowl
11. little
12. pebbles; beetles
13. change

JANUARY AUTHORS BIBLIOGRAPHY

January 1   Barbara Williams

Albert's Toothache, illustrated by Kay Chorao (Dutton, 1974); *Kevin's Grandma* (Dutton, 1975); *Chester Chipmunk's Thanksgiving* (Dutton, 1978); *Jeremy Isn't Hungry*, illustrated by Martha Alexander (Dutton, 1978); *Horrible, Impossible, Bad Witch Child* (Avon, 1982); *Mitzi & the Terrible Tyrannosaurus Rex* (Dutton, 1982); *Mitzi's Honeymoon with Nana Potts* (Dutton, 1983); *Mitzi & Frederick the Great* (Dutton, 1984).

January 2   Isaac Asimov

He has written over 300 books and stories in his long and wonderful career as a writer. For good third grade readers, Avon Camelot series: How did we find out about—Antarctica, Atoms, Black Holes, Comets, Computers, Dinosaurs, etc.

January 2   Crosby Bonsall

Who's a Pest (Harper, 1962); *It's Mine* (Harper, 1964); *Mine's the Best* (Harper, 1973); *And I Mean It, Stanley* (Harper, 1974); *Amazing, the Incredible Super Dog* (Harper, 1986); I-Can-Read books published by Trophy: *The Case of the Cat's Meow, The Case of the Double Cross, The Case of the Dumb Bells, The Case of the Hungry Stranger, The Case of the Scaredy Cats.*

January 3   Joan Walsh Anglund

In a Pumpkin Shell: A Mother Goose ABC (HBJ, 1960); *Christmas Is a Time of Giving* (HBJ, 1961); *Emily and Adam* (Random House, 1979); *Childhood Is a Time of Innocence* (HBJ, 1984); *Christmas Is Here* (HBJ, 1986).

January 3   Carolyn Haywood

A Valentine Fantasy (Morrow, 1976); *The King's Monster* (Morrow, 1980); *Santa Claus Forever!* (Morrow, 1983); *How the Reindeer Saved Santa* (Morrow, 1986); *Two and Two Are Four* (HBJ, 1986); Betsy series: *B Is for Betsy, Back to School with Betsy*; Eddie series: *Ever Ready Eddie, Eddie the Dog Holder*—perfect for second grade readers who want easy but longer books, published by HBJ.

January 4   Beverly Fiday

Jeff's Happy Day (Standard, 1984); *Ears, Eyes, Nose, and Mouth* (Standard, 1985); *Patience: What Is It?* (Child's World, 1985); *Respect: What Is It?* (Child's World, 1988); *Time to Go* (HBJ, scheduled for 1990).

January 4   Jacob Grimm

Famous writer of fairy tales, including: *Elves and the Shoemaker, Cinderella, Fisherman and His Wife, Golden Goose, Hansel and Gretel.*

January Authors Bibliography

January 4   Fernando Krahn

Illustrator of very funny wordless picture books: *April Fools* (Dutton, 1974); *Little Love Story* (Lippincott, 1976); *Mystery of the Giant's Footprints* (Dutton, 1977); *The Creepy Thing* (Houghton Mifflin, 1982); *Secret in the Dungeon* (Houghton Mifflin, 1983); *Amanda and the Mysterious Carpet* (Houghton Mifflin, 1985).

January 6   Carl Sandburg

Wind Song (HBJ, 1960); *Sandburg Treasury* (HBJ, 1970); *Rootabaga Stories* (HBJ, 1974); *Early Moon* (HBJ, 1978).

January 7   Eleanor Clymer

For good third grade readers: *Chipmuck in the Forest* (Macmillan, 1972); *Search for Two Bad Mice* (Macmillan, 1980); *Horatio* (Macmillan, 1985); *Horatio's Birthday* (Macmillan, 1985); *Horse in the Attic* (Dell, 1985); *Trolley Car Family* (Scholastic, 1987).

January 7   Kay Chorao

Has illustrated the best works of others, as well as her own stories: *Molly's Moe* (Houghton Mifflin, 1979); *Oink & Pearl* (Harper, 1981); *Ups & Downs with Oink and Pearl* (Harper, 1986); *George Told Kate* (Dutton, 1987); preschool titles published by Dutton: *Kate's Box, Car, Quilt,* and *Snowman.*

January 8   Lee J. Ames

Draw 50 series published by Doubleday: *Draw 50 Dinosaurs, Draw 50 Vehicles, Draw 50 Monsters, Draw 50 Horses, Draw 50 Cars, Draw 50 Buildings,* etc.

January 9   Clyde Robert Bulla

Sword in the Tree (Crowell, 1956); *Lincoln's Birthday* (Harper, 1966); *Ghost of Windy Hill* (Crowell, 1968); *Wish at the Top* (Crowell, 1974); *Keep Running, Allen!* (Harper, 1978); *Daniel's Duck* (Harper, 1979); *My Friend the Monster* (Harper, 1980); *Charlie's House* (Harper, 1983); *Cardboard Crown* (Harper, 1984); Chalk Box Kid (Random House, 1987).

January 10   Remy Charlip

Fortunately (Macmillan, 1985).

January 12   Clement Hurd

Illustrated: *Goodnight, Moon* by Margaret Brown (Harper, 1947); Johnny Lion books by Edith Hurd (Harper, 1970s); *Runaway Bunny* by Margaret Brown (Harper, 1972).

January 12   Charles Perrault

Cinderella (Penguin, 1977); *Perrault's Complete Fairy Tales* (Dodd, 1982).

January 13   N. M. Bodecker

Let's Marry Said the Cherry (Macmillan, out of print); *It's Raining, Said John Twaining* (Macmillan, 1977); *Mushroom Center Disaster* (Macmillan, 1979); *Carrot Holes and Frisbee Trees* (Atheneum, 1983); *Hurry, Hurry, Mary Dear* (Macmillan, 1987).

January 15   William Arden

For good third grade readers. He wrote many of the books in the Alfred Hitchcock and the three investigators series published by Random House: *Mystery of the Moaning Cave, Shark Reef*, and *Purple Pirate*; plus 13 others.

January 17   John Bellairs

For good third grade readers: *House with a Clock in Its Walls* (Dial, 1974); *The Letter, the Witch, and the Ring* (Dial, 1977); *Curse of the Blue Figurine* (Dial, 1983); *The Mummy, the Will, and the Crypt* (Dial, 1983); *Revenge of the Wizard's Ghost* (Dial, 1985).

January 18   Raymond Briggs

Wordless stories that children will love to talk to you about: *Father Christmas* (Putnam, 1973); *The Snowman* (Random, 1986); *Fairy Tale Treasury* (Dell, 1986).

January 18   A. A. Milne

On a dreary day or under a tree, these stories should be a memory of each child's early school days: *World of Christopher Robin* (Dutton, 1958); *Now We Are Six* (Dutton, 1961); *When We Were Very Young* (Dutton, 1961); *House at Pooh Corner* (Dell, 1970).

January 18   Arthur Ransome

The Fool of the World and His Flying Ship (Farrar, 1968)—1969 Caldecott Award winner.

January 22   Margaret Hillert

Over 30 titles available from Follett Library Book Company and Story House Corporation. First grade easy reading series of 1.1 to 1.9 reading levels.

January 22   Blair Lent

Baba Yaga (Houghton Mifflin, 1966); *Why the Sun & Moon Live in the Sky* (Houghton Mifflin, 1968)—1969 Caldecott Honor book; illustrated *The Funny Little Woman* by Arlene Mosel (Dutton, 1972)—1973 Caldecott Award winner, out of print; *Bayberry Bluff* (Houghton Mifflin, 1987).

January 22   Brian Wildsmith

Boldly colored kindergarten books published by Oxford University Press: *Animal Homes, Animal Shapes, Animal Tricks, Birds, the Circus; Bear's*

Adventure (Pantheon, 1982); *Pelican* (Pantheon, 1983); *Daisy* (Pantheon, 1984); *Give a Dog a Bone* (Pantheon, 1985); *Goat's Tail* (Knopf, 1986).

January 27   Lewis Carroll

Alice in Wonderland (Scholastic, 1985); *Jabberwocky* (Whitman, 1985); *Through the Looking Glass & What Alice Found There* (Knopf, 1986).

January 27   Harry Allard

First and second grade readers will love these: *Bumps in the Night* (Bantam, 1984); *There's a Party at Mona's Tonight* (Avon, 1985); Miss Nelson series published by Houghton Mifflin: *Miss Nelson Is Missing, Miss Nelson Is Back, Miss Nelson Has a Field Day*; The Stupids series published by Houghton Mifflin: *The Stupids Step Out, The Stupids Have a Ball*.

January 29   Bill Peet

All titles are published by Houghton Mifflin: *Kermit the Hermit* (1965); *Capyboppy* (1966); *Countdown to Christmas* (1972); *Big Bad Bruce* (1978); *Chester the Worldly Pig* (1978); *How Droofus the Dragon Lost His Head* (1983).

January 29   Rosemary Wells

All titles are published by Dial: *Morris' Disappearing Bag: A Chrishtmas Story* (1978); *Noisy Nora* (1980); *Max's Bath* (1985); *Max's Birthday* (1985); *Max's Breakfast* (1985).

January 30   Tony Johnston

Happy Birthday Mole and Troll (Putnam, 1979—out of print); *Night Noises and Other Mole and Troll Stories* (out of print); *Mole and Troll Trim the Tree* (out of print); *Four Scary Stories* (Putnam, 1980); *Odd Jobs and Friends* (Putnam, 1982); *The Vanishing Pumpkin* (Putnam, 1983); *The Witch's Hat* (Putnam, 1984); *The Quilt Story* (Putnam, 1985); *Farmer Mack Measures His Pig* (Harper, 1986); *Five Little Foxes and the Snow* (Harper, 1987); *Yonder* (Dial, 1988).

January 31   Gerald McDermott

Arrow to the Sun (Viking, 1974)—1975 Caldecott Award winner; *The Stonecutter* (Penguin, 1978); *Sun Flight* (Macmillan, 1980); *Daughter of the Earth: A Roman Myth* (Delacorte, 1984); *Daniel O'Rourke* (Viking, 1986); *Tim O'Toole & the Little People* (Viking, 1987).

 # FEBRUARY

February 3   Joan Lowrey Nixon, *The Valentine Mystery* (mystery words)

February 4   Russell Hoban, *Bread and Jam for Frances* (junk food questions)

February 8   Adrienne Adams, *The Shoemaker and the Elves* (writing activity)

February 9   Dick Gackenbach, *Harry and the Terrible Whatzit* (fill in)

February 11   Jane Yolen, *Owl Moon* (fill in)

February 12   Judy Blume, *The One in the Middle Is a Green Kangaroo* (fill in)

February 14   Send a valentine to your favorite author (drawing/writing activity)

February 15   Mike Thaler, *There's a Hippopotamus Under My Bed* (writing activity)

February 15   Norman Bridwell, *Witch Next Door* (writing activity)

February 20   David Fiday, *Time to Go* (short-answer questions)

              David Fiday, "Send Me a Note" writing activity

February 24   Wilhelm Grimm, *Snow White* (fill in)

February 27   Florence Parry Heide, *The Shrinking of Treehorn* (short-answer questions)

February 27   Uri Shulevitz, *The Treasure* (short-answer questions)

  February Bookmarks
  February Answer Key
  February Authors Bibliography

FEBRUARY AUTHORS

DATE	NAME	AUTHOR/ILLUSTRATOR		READING LEVEL			
				K	1	2	3
2	Rebecca Caudill	X				X	X
2	Judith Viorst	X			X	X	
3	Joan Lowery Nixon	X				X	X
4	Russell Hoban	X			X	X	
7	Charles Dickens	X					X
7	Laura Ingalls Wilder	X					X
8	Adrienne Adams	X	X			X	X
8	Anne Rockwell	X	X	X	X		
9	Dick Gackenbach	X	X	X	X	X	
10	Franz Brandenberg	X	X	X	X	X	
11	Jane Yolen	X		X	X	X	
12	Judy Blume	X				X	X
15	Norman Bridwell	X	X	X	X	X	
15	Mike Thaler	X			X	X	X
16	Edward Packard	X				X	X
17	Robert Newton Peck	X					X
19	Louis Slobodkin	X					X
20	Mary Blount Christian	X			X	X	X
20	David Fiday	X				X	X
24	Wilhelm Grimm	X				X	X
27	Florence Parry Heide	X				X	X
27	Uri Shulevitz	X	X	X	X	X	X
27	Henry Wadsworth Longfellow	X				X	X
28	Sir John Tenniel		X				

JOAN LOWREY NIXON

"The Valentine Mystery"

Read "The Valentine Mystery." Answer the Who, What, Where, How, and Why questions about this mystery.

1. Who answered the door? _____.

2. What clue did he give Susan? _____.

3. Where did Pete have buckles? _____.

4. What did Barney call every shoe or boot? _____.

5. What did Susan remember about Pete's boots?

_____

Now you know the answer to the Valentine Mystery. Send a mystery Valentine of your own. Don't let anyone know who you are. See if they can guess who sent it. Make it yourself.

Name _____ **Date** _____

RUSSELL HOBAN

"Bread and Jam for Frances"

Read "Bread and Jam for Frances," Answer the questions about your favorite "junk food" snack.

1. What is your favorite "junk food"?

_____

2. What is the best time to eat your snack?

_____

3. How do you make your snack ready to eat? List the steps.

_____

_____

_____

_____

4. What could you eat instead of your "junk food"?

_____

_____

_____

Name_____ **Date**_____

ADRIENNE ADAMS

"The Shoemaker and the Elves"

Read "The Shoemaker and the Elves." The Grimm Brothers wrote the story, but Adrienne Adams drew the pictures.

Every night as the shoemaker slept, little elves helped him do his work. When the shoemaker woke up, he had a "sweet surprise." A sweet surprise is a little help you don't expect.

Fill in this sheet with the names of people and what sweet surprises you could give them. If you're sweet enough, you could do the surprises for them.

PERSON   SURPRISE

_____   _____

_____   _____

_____   _____

_____   _____

_____   _____

_____   _____

_____   _____

_____   _____

_____   _____

_____   _____

_____   _____

Name_____   **Date**_____

DICK GACKENBACH

"Harry and the Terrible Whatzit"

Read "Harry and the Terrible Whatzit." Use the words in the Word Bank to finish these setences about a brave little boy who chases his fear out of the cellar.

1. Harry didn't like the _____ and _____ cellar.

2. He took a _____ and went after the _____.

3. It was behind the _____.

4. It had two _____.

5. When Harry hit it, the Whatzit got _____.

6. Harry twisted its _____.

7. The thing became smaller because Harry wasn't _____.

8. Harry sent the Whatzit _____ _____.

9. Harry found his mother's _____ on the shelf.

10. He went out into the back _____.

11. Mom was picking _____.

12. Harry heard a _____ from next door.

WORD BANK

afraid	broom	damp	dark	flowers	furnace
heads	glasses	next door	smaller	tail	Whatzit
yard	yell				

DRAW A PICTURE OF THE WHATZIT YOU ONCE SAW ON THE BACK OF THIS PAGE. THEY COME IN ALL SIZES AND SHAPES YOU KNOW!

Name _____   **Date** _____

JANE YOLEN

"Owl Moon"

Read "Owl Moon." Use the words in the Word Bank to finish these sentences about the Caldecott story of looking for owls late at night.

1. One winter _____ we went _____.

2. The trees were like giant _____.

3. The night was as quiet as a _____.

4. My shadow was short and _____.

5. Papa made the sound of the Great _____ owl.

6. We stood in a _____ in the dark woods.

7. Suddenly, a _____ of the tree branch moved.

8. The owl _____ again.

9. The owl landed on a _____.

10. We _____ at one another.

11. Then the owl _____ its strong wings.

12. Off it _____. My owling was _____.

WORD BANK						
branch	clearing	dream	flew	hooted	Horned	night
over	owling	pumped	round	shadow	stared	statues

Name_____ **Date**_____

JUDY BLUME

"The One in the Middle Is a Green Kangaroo"

Read "The One in the Middle Is a Green Kangaroo." Use the words in the Word Bank to finish these sentences about how Freddy HOPS out of his problem.

1. Freddy didn't like being in the _____.

2. He got Mike's old _____.

3. Ellen got Freddy's _____.

4. Freddy wanted to be in the school _____.

5. He hopped around the _____.

6. He got the part of the green _____.

7. Mike choked on his _____.

8. Ellen _____ at the spilled milk.

9. Freddy _____ for two weeks.

10. Ms. Gumber told him to "_____ a _____."

11. Freddy was _____, but he knew he had a _____ to do.

12. In the end, Freddy felt just _____ about being Freddy Diesel.

WORD BANK				
afraid	break	clothes	great	job
kangaroo	laughed	leg	middle	play
potato	practiced	room	stage	

Name _____ Date _____

FEBRUARY 14

Valentine's Day

Let's celebrate Valentine's Day in a special way. Pick one of the following activities.

1. Pick your favorite book from the library. Design and make a new book jacket for the book.

   a. Make a beautiful cover. It could be your favorite scene or pictures of your favorite character.

   b. Write a short summary of the book for the back. Include why you liked the book so much. Mention your favorite scene. But don't give away the ending. Some people like to be surprised when they read a book.

   c. Ask your librarian or media specialist to laminate it for you.

2. Make a valentine card for your favorite author or illustrator. Send it to him or her. Most authors accept mail through their publisher. You can find the addresses of publishers on company catalogs.

3. If you haven't read "A Valentine Fantasy" by Carolyn Haywood do so today. Write her a thank you Valentine for such a sweet, sweet story.

4. Make a Valentine for anybody you love. Let everyone know you CARE about them. But most of all, make sure you enjoy the day too!

Name _____   Date _____

MIKE THALER

"There's a Hippopotamus Under My Bed"

Read "There's a Hippopotamus Under My Bed." The little boy has a problem with an escaped hippo. But how would the story have been different if he found one of these animals?

PEACOCK

SKUNK

MOOSE

SNAKE

Write a story about the time you found one of these animals. Think about these questions before you start your story.

Where did you find your animal?

What did your friends say?

What did your parents say?

What did the animal do to your house?

What did you say when the zoo keepers came to take it back?

Write your story on the next page.

Name _____   Date _____

MIKE THALER

"Writing Activity"

There's a _____ Under My Bed

© 1989 by The Center for Applied Research in Education

_____

_____

_____

_____

_____

_____

_____

_____

_____

_____

_____

_____

_____

_____

_____

Name_____   **Date**_____

NORMAN BRIDWELL

"Witch Next Door"

Read "The Witch Next Door." Not everyone is lucky enough to live next door to a witch. But guess who just moved in next to you? A witch!

If you had a witch for a next-door neighbor, what would you ask her to do? Write a story about you and your new friend.

Think about these questions before you write your story.

How did you meet her?

What does she look like? Does she look like a witch?

Did she need your help first?

Why did she move to your neighborhood?

Where does she fly you on her broom?

What do you help her cook in her pot?

Does she have any special pets?

What does her pet do that is strange and different?

WRITE YOUR STORY ON THE NEXT PAGE.

Name_____ **Date**_____

"MY FRIEND THE WITCH"

by

_____

Name_____ **Date**_____

BEVERLY & DAVID FIDAY

"Time to Go"

___

Read "Time to Go." This is a story of change. The little boy is leaving his farm. He is very sad to do that, but there isn't anything he can do about leaving. But he can take his memories with him.

Imagine you are leaving home. Perhaps your dad has a new job. Maybe your mother earned a promotion. Answer these questions to help you write your own "Time to Go."

Where are you living now? _____.

What activities do you enjoy most in your backyard, in the park, at a friend's, any special places in or around your house. Use the back of this paper for more things you like to do.

_____

_____

_____

_____

_____

How will you get to your new house? _____.

What one thing will you never forget?

_____

Do you think you'll ever go back? _____.

Why or why not?

_____

_____

Name_____ **Date**_____

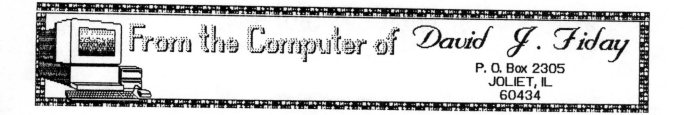

Hi Kids!

Now's your chance to talk to me. I've worked so many hours on getting all these activities done for you. I hope you and your teacher enjoy them.

Did I leave out any of your favorite authors, illustrators, or poets? If I have, I want you to do me a favor.

a. Write me a note telling me the name of your favorite author, illustrator, or poet. If he or she isn't in the book, there is a simple reason. I don't know his or her birthday. If you send me their name and birthdate, I'll include it in the next revision of this book. And I'll make sure you're given the credit for finding that person being included.

b. Send your postcard to the address above. I'll send you a thank you note.

Name_____ **Date**_____

WILHELM GRIMM

"Snow White"

Read "Snow White." Use the words in the Word Bank to finish these sentences about a young princess who is an innocent victim of a wicked stepmother.

1. One winter day, a queen wished for a _____.

2. When her wish was granted, she _____.

3. The king married a new _____.

4. This one had a magic _____.

5. The queen wanted to be the most _____ one.

6. One day, the mirror said _____ was prettiest.

7. The queen wanted her _____.

8. The hunstman brought back a _____ lung and liver.

9. Snow White found a house owned by _____.

10. The queen tied Snow White's laces too _____.

11. She gave Snow White a poison _____.

12. She gave Snow White a _____ apple.

13. A _____ found and married Snow White.

```
WORD BANK
beautiful      boar's      child      comb      died      dwarfs
killed         mirror      queen      poison    prince    Snow White
tight
```

Name_____   Date_____

FLORENCE PARRY HEIDE

"The Shrinking of Treehorn"

Read "The Shrinking of Treehorn." It is a sad story because Treehorn shrinks. He shrinks because he is ignored. Everyone hates to be ignored. It makes us feel small and unimportant. And that is sad. Answer these questions and talk to your mom and dad about them. It's important to talk, especially to parents.

1. When do you feel the smallest? the most ignored?

   _____

2. Do you ignore brothers and sisters? _____.

   When _____

   _____

3. Can you name three ways to make friends and family feel very BIG?

   _____

   _____

   _____

4. The next time someone makes you feel small, unimportant, or like "small potatoes"— let them know how you feel.

REMEMBER: NO MATTER HOW PEOPLE HURT YOUR FEELINGS—YOU ARE LOVED!

Even if others forget about you
For every wonderful thing you do,
I thank you and *LOVE* you, too!

Name_____ Date_____

URI SHULEVITZ

"The Treasure"

Read "The Treasure." This beautifully illustrated story was named a Caldecott Honor book. It is the story of a man who travels far "to find his treasure at home", just as Dorothy did in the *Wizard of Oz*. Let's look into your home and see what treasures you have.

1. How are your parents treasures?

_____

_____

2. How are brothers or sisters treasures?

_____

_____

3. Can grandparents be treasures? How?

_____

_____

4. There are other treasures too: friends, teachers, bus drivers, people in your church. Can strangers be treasures too? How can that be?

PICK ONE KIND OF PERSON FROM NUMBER 4. WRITE ON THE BACK OF THIS SHEET HOW YOU THINK THEY CAN BE TREASURES. WRITE THE BEST EXAMPLES THAT COME TO MIND.

P.S.: Students who love to read or listen to a great story are TREASURES for me!

Name_____ Date_____

february

readers love books!

we love

books!

books are

our best friends

 i'll keep your place

til spring comes!

 **PRESIDENTS**

READERS ARE LEADERS

FEBRUARY ANSWER KEY

JOAN LOWREY NIXON: *The Valentine Mystery*

1. Barney
2. He had watches on his tennis shoes
3. On his boots
4. Tennis shoes
5. They had buckles that looked like watches.

DICK GACKENBACH: *Harry and the Terrible Whatzit*

1. dark; damp
2. broom; Whatzit
3. furnace
4. heads
5. smaller
6. tail
7. afraid
8. next door
9. glasses
10. yard
11. flowers
12. yell

JANE YOLEN: *Owl Moon*

1. night; owling
2. statues
3. dream
4. round
5. Horned
6. clearing
7. shadow
8. hooted
9. branch
10. stared
11. pumped
12. flew; over

JUDY BLUME: *The One in the Middle Is a Green Kangaroo*

1. middle
2. clothes
3. room
4. play
5. stage
6. kangaroo
7. potato
8. laughed
9. practiced
10. break; leg
11. afraid; job
12. great

WILHELM GRIMM: *Snow White*

1. child
2. died
3. queen
4. mirror
5. beautiful
6. Snow White
7. killed
8. boar's
9. dwarfs
10. tight
11. comb
12. poison
13. prince

FEBRUARY AUTHORS BIBLIOGRAPHY

February 2   Rebecca Caudill

Pocketful of Cricket (Holt, 1964)—1965 Caldecott Honor book; *A Certain Small Shepard* (Holt, 1965); *Wind, Sand, & Sky* (Dutton, 1976).

February 2   Judith Viorst

Tenth Good Thing About Barney (Atheneum, 1971); *Alexander and the Terrible, Horrible, No Good, Very Bad Day* (Macmillan, 1972); *My Mama Says There Aren't Any Zombies, Ghosts, Creatures, Demons, Monsters, Fiends, Goblins, or Things* (Macmillan, 1973); *Alexander Who Used to Be Rich Last Sunday* (Macmillan, 1978); *If I Were in Charge of the World & Other Worries* (Macmillan, 1984).

February 3   Joan Lowery Nixon

Second and third grade reading mystery series about holidays published by Whitman: *New Year's Eve Mystery, Christmas Eve Mystery, April Fool Mystery, Thanksgiving Mystery, Valentine Mystery, Happy Birthday Mystery*; *Bigfoot Makes a Movie* (Scholastic, 1983); *Beats Me, Claude* (Viking, 1986); *Fat Chance, Claude* (Viking, date not set).

February 4   Russell Hoban

Bedtime for Frances (Harper, 1960); *Bread and Jam for Frances* (Harper, 1964); *Baby Sister for Frances* (Harper, 1964); *Tom and the Two Handles* (Harper, 1965); *Best Friends for Frances* (Harper, 1969); *Bargain for Frances* (Harper, 1970); *Dinner at Alberta's* (Crowell, 1975); *A Birthday for Frances* (Harper, 1976); *Charlie Meadows* (Holt, 1984); *Jim Frog* (Holt, 1984); *The Little Brute Family* (Avon, 1986); *The Stone Doll of Sister Brute* (Avon, 1986).

February 7   Charles Dickens

The Best-loved Dickens tale for the under-10 set: *A Christmas Carol* (Creative Education, 1983); *A Christmas Carol* (Ideals, 1985)—for Grades K-6; *A Christmas Carol* (Macmillan, 1986)—a pop-up book.

February 7   Laura Ingalls Wilder

Little House series is a moving and marvelous set of tales of America's history as seen through the eyes of a young girl. Some children, especially girls, start reading these books in third grade. The series is published by Harper: *Little House on the Prairie, Little Town on the Prairie, Little House in the Big Woods, Farmer Boy, The Long Winter*, etc.

February Authors Bibliography

February 8   Adrienne Adams

Houses from the Sea (1960 Caldecott Honor Book—out of print); *Woggle of Witches* (Macmillan, 1971); *Christmas Party* (Macmillan, 1978); *Easter Egg Artists* (Macmillan, 1981); *A Halloween Happening* (Macmillan, 1981); *The Shoemaker and the Elves* (Macmillan, 1981); *Christmas Party* (Macmillan, 1982); *The Great Valentine's Day Balloon Race* (Macmillan, 1986).

February 8   Anne Rockwell

These preK-K concept books can double as easy-to-read books for first graders. Many titles have big, beautiful illustrations: *Toolbox* (Macmillan, 1971); *Machines* (Macmillan, 1972); *Our Garage Sale* (Greenwillow, 1984); *In the Morning, In Our House, In the Rain* (Crowell, 1985).

February 9   Dick Gackenbach

Claude & Pepper (Houghton Mifflin, 1976); *Hound & Bear* (Houghton Mifflin, 1976); *Hattie Rabbit* (Harper, 1977); *Hattie Be Quiet, Hattie Be Good* (Harper, 1977); *Harry and the Terrible Whatzit* (Houghton Mifflin, 1978); *More Hound & Bear* (Houghton Mifflin, 1979); *Claude the Dog* (Houghton Mifflin, 1982).

February 10   Franz Brandenberg

Nice New Neighbors (Greenwillow, 1977); *Leo and Emily* (Greenwillow, 1982); *Leo and Emily and the Dragon* (Greenwillow, 1982); *Leo and Emily's Big Ideas* (Greenwillow, 1982); *Aunt Nina and Her Nephews and Nieces* (Greenwillow, 1984); *Aunt Nina's Visit* (Greenwillow, 1984); *The Hit of the Party* (Greenwillow, 1988).

February 11   Jane Yolen

Commander Toad series published by Putnam: *CT in Space and the Disasteroid, CT and the Big Black Hole, CT and the Intergalatic Spy, CT and the Planet of the Grapes, CT and the Space Pirates*; *The Girl Who Loved the Wind* (Harper, 1972); *The Rainbow Rider* (Harper, 1974); *No Bath Tonight* (Harper, 1978); *Piggins* (HBJ, 1987); *Owl Moon* (Putnam, 1987)—1988 Caldecott Award winner.

February 12   Judy Blume

Freckle Juice (Macmillan, 1971); *Tales of a Fourth-Grade Nothing* (Dutton, 1972); *Superfudge* (Dutton, 1980); *The Pain and the Great One* (Bradbury, 1984); *The One in the Middle Is a Green Kangaroo* (Dell, 1986).

February 15   Mike Thaler

Stuffed Feet (Scholastic, 1983); *Funny Side Up* (Scholastic, 1985); *Cream of Creature from the School Cafeteria* (Avon, 1985); *King Kong's Underwear* (Avon, 1986); *Madge's Magic Show* (Avon, 1986); *There's a Hippopotamus Under My Bed* (Avon, 1986); *A Hippopotamus Ate the Teacher* (Avon, 1986); *Scared Silly* (Avon, 1986).

February Authors Bibliography

February 15   Norman Bridwell

Popular series published by Scholastic: *Clifford the Big Red Dog, Clifford's Kitten, Clifford's Riddles, Clifford Gets a Job, Clifford at the Circus, Clifford the Small Red Puppy*; *Witch Next Door* (Scholastic, 1986); *Witch's Catalog* (Scholastic, 1986); *Witch's Christmas* (Scholastic, 1986).

February 16   Edward Packard

King of "Choose Your Own" Third Planet from Altair, and many others. ESP McGee mystery series published by Avon: *ESP McGee and the Dolphin's Message, ESP McGee and the Ghost Ship, ESP McGee and the Haunted Mansion, ESP McGee and the Mysterious Magician, ESP McGee to the Rescue.*

February 17   Robert Newton Peck

Many great "Soup" books to read aloud, published by Delacorte: *Soup and Me, Soup on Wheels, Soup for President, Soup on Ice, Soup in the Saddle, Soup's Drum, Soup's Goat, Soup on Fire*; Trig series especially for girls who love humor, published by Dell or Little Brown: *Trig, Trig Sees Red, Trig Goes Ape, Trig or Treat.*

February 19   Louis Slobodkin

Many Moons (HBJ, 1943; illustrated by Slobodkin, written by James Thurber)—1944 Caldecott Award winner; *Magic Michael* (Macmillan, 1968); boxed set published by Macmillan in 1981: *Spaceship Under the Apple Tree, Spaceship Returns to the Apple Tree, Three-Seated Spaceship.*

February 20   Mary Blount Christian

Doggone Mystery (Whitman, 1980); *Two Ton Secret* (Whitman, 1981); *Green Thumb Thief* (Whitman, 1982); *Undercover Kids and the Museum Mystery* (Whitman, 1983); Sebastian Super Sleuth series published by Macmillan, 1986: *SS & the Bone to Pick Mystery, SS & the Crummy Yummies Caper, SS & the Hair of the Dog Mystery, SS & the Purloined Sirloin, SS & the Secret of the Skewered Skier, SS & the Clumsy Cowboy, SS & the Santa Claus Caper.*

February 20   David Fiday

Ears, Eyes, Nose, Mouth (Standard, 1986); *Sweet Surprises* (Standard, 1989); *Time to Go*, coauthored with Beverly Fiday (HBJ, set for 1990).

February 24   Wilhelm Grimm

Helped his brother, Jacob, compile German fairy tales. See "January 4, Jacob Grimm" for a complete listing.

February 27   Florence Parry Heide

Shrinking of Treehorn, Treehorn's Treasure, Treehorn's Wish, Adventures of Treehorn (Dell, 1983); *Banana Blitz, Banana Twist* (Holiday House, 1984). Coauthored Brillstone mystery books with Roxanne Heide for good third grade readers: *Face at the Brillstone Window, Brillstone Break-In, Body in the Brillstone Garage.* Easy-to-read mysteries from Whitman grades 2–3: *Mystery of the Forgotten Island, Melting Snowman, Midnight Message, Mummy's Mask, Vanishing Visitor.*

February 27   Uri Shulevitz

Illustrator of *The Fool of the World and His Flying Ship* (Farrar, 1968)—1969 Caldecott Award winner; *The Treasure* (Farrar, 1979)—1980 Caldecott Honor Book; *Dawn* (Farrar, 1974); *One Monday Morning* (Macmillan, 1986) paperback.

February 27   Henry Wadsworth Longfellow

"Jemima" from *Beastly Boys and Ghastly Girls*, collected by William Cole (World, 1964); *Hiawatha*, illustrated by Susan Jeffers (Dial, 1983); *Paul Revere's Ride* (Greenwillow, 1985).

February 28   Sir John Tenniel

Original illustrator of *Lewis Carroll: The Complete Works* (Merrimack, 1978).

MARCH

March 2	Leo Dillon, *Why Mosquitoes Buzz in People's Ears* (scrambled words)
March 2	Dr. Seuss (Theodore Geisel), *Bartholomew and the Oobleck* (fill in)
	Dr. Seuss (Theodore Geisel), *On Beyond Zebra* (fantasy)
March 6	Thacher Hurd, *Mystery on the Docks* (mystery words)
March 8	Edna Miller, *Mousekin Takes a Trip* (word meanings)
March 10	Jack Kent, *The Once-Upon-a-Time Dragon* (story sequence)
March 11	Ezra Jack Keats, *Peter's Chair* (scrambled words)
March 16	Sid Fleischman, *McBroom's Ghost* (fill in)
March 20	Mitsumasa Anno, *Anno's Alphabet* and *Anno's Counting Book* (for the teacher)
March 21	Margaret Mahy, *The Boy Who Was Followed Home* (writing)
March 22	Harry Devlin, *Cranberry Mystery* (wordsearch)
March 26	Robert Frost, *You Come Too: Favorite Poems for Young Readers* (short-answer fill-in)

March Bookmarks
March Answer Key
March Authors Bibliography

MARCH AUTHORS

DATE	NAME	AUTHOR/ILLUSTRATOR		READING LEVEL			
				K	1	2	3
1	Lonzo Anderson	X		X	X	X	
2	Leo Dillon		X				
2	Dr. Seuss	X	X	X	X	X	X
6	Thacher Hurd	X	X	X	X	X	
8	Edna Miller	X		X	X	X	
9	Joan M. Lexau	X				X	X
10	Jack Kent	X	X	X	X	X	
11	Wanda Gag	X	X	X	X	X	
11	Ezra Jack Keats	X	X	X	X	X	
13	Diane Dillon		X				
16	Sid Fleischman	X				X	X
17	Kate Greenaway		X	X	X	X	X
20	Mitsumasa Anno	X	X	X	X		
21	Phyllis McGinley	X			X	X	X
21	Margaret Mahy	X			X	X	X
22	Randolph Caldecott		X				
22	Harry Devlin	X	X	X	X	X	
23	Eleanor Cameron	X					X
26	Robert Frost	X				X	X
26	Betty MacDonald	X					X
30	Charles Keller	X			X	X	X
31	Beni Montresor		X	X	X	X	

LEO & DIANE DILLON

"Why Mosquitoes Buzz in People's Ears"

Read "Why Mosquitoes Buzz in People's Ears" illustrated by Leo and Diane Dillon. Use the words in the Word Bank to unscramble the names of the animals below.

1. STOOMUQI   __ __ __ __ __ __ __ __

2. NAGUAI   __ __ __ __ __ __

3. THONPY   __ __ __ __ __ __

4. BARTIB   __ __ __ __ __ __

5. NOKMEY   __ __ __ __ __ __

6. LOW   __ __ __

7. NOLI   __ __ __ __

8. PEELATON   __ __ __ __ __ __ __ __

9. WROC   __ __ __ __

10. THNAPEEL   __ __ __ __ __ __ __ __

WORD BANK

antelope	crow	elephant	iguana	lion
monkey	mosquito	owl	python	rabbit

Name_____   Date_____

DR. SEUSS

"Bartholomew and the Oobleck"

Read "Bartholomew and the Oobleck." Use the words in the Word Bank to finish the sentences below.

1. The King lived in the land of _____.

2. The King was tired of four things that fell from the sky _____, _____, _____, and _____.

3. The King called for his _____.

4. They promised to make _____.

5. It was as sticky as _____.

6. The King's _____ was stuck to his head.

7. Bartholomew told the King to say he was _____.

8. The simple magic word _____ the Oobleck away.

WORD BANK

chased	crown	Didd	fog	glue	king
magicians	Oobleck	rain	snow	sorry	sunshine

Name_____   Date_____

DR. SEUSS

"On Beyond Zebra"

Read "On Beyond Zebra." In this story, Dr. Seuss creates a fantasy (unreal) alphabet. If you look closely at the letters, you can discover how he did it. Let's use the UM as an example.

The letter UM is the letter U sitting on top of the letter M. UM is the first sound in the word Umbus.

The letter Zatz is a Z with a T on the end. The FLOOB is the letter F with a B wedged in the middle.

1. Create your own letter. What word begins with that letter?

2. Can you define the word? Is it the name of an animal you know? Is it a verb (action word)?

3. In the frame below, draw a picture to go with the word.

There are more fantasy letters from Dr. Seuss' fantasy alphabet on the next page.

Name _____   Date _____

DR. SEUSS

"On Beyond Zebra"

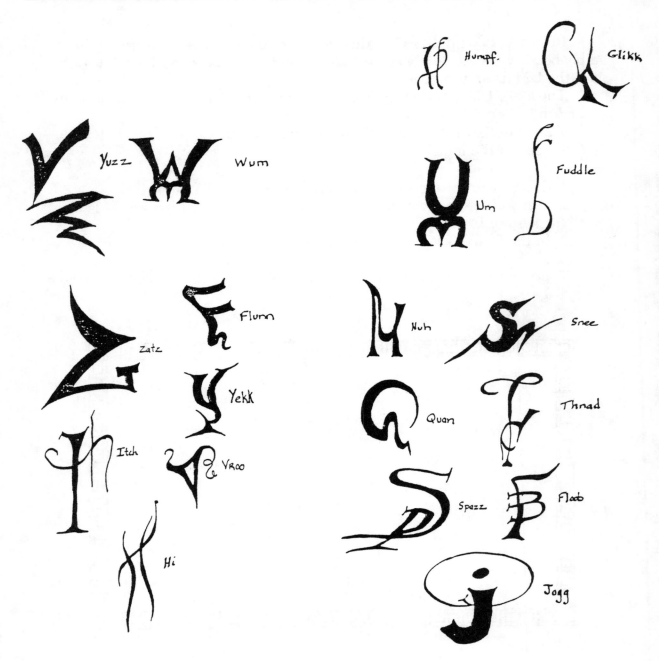

Reprinted with permission from *On Beyond Zebra* by Dr. Seuss (Random House, Inc. © 1955).

THACHER HURD

"Mystery on the Docks"

Read "Mystery on the Docks." Mysteries always contain five important words: who, what, where, when, and why. Answer the five important questions below.

1. Who solved the mystery of the kidnapping?

_____

2. What did the newspaper say the mystery was about?

_____

_____

3. Where was the mystery solved?

_____

4. When did Ralph first know something strange was happening?

_____

5. Why was Eduardo Bombasto kidnapped by Big Al?

_____

Name_____ Date_____

EDNA MILLER

"Mousekin Takes a Trip"

Read "Mousekin Takes a Trip." Mousekin visits the desert and sees many animals.
Use the words in the Word Bank to help you fill in the words to match their meanings.

1. __ __ __ __ __ __ __   mobile house

2. __ __ __ __ __ __   sandy land

3. __ __ __ __ __ __   thorny plant

4. __ __ __ __ __ __   slender reptile with tail

5. __ __ __ __ __ __ __ __   turtle cousin

6. __ __ __ __ __ __ __   kind of cactus

7. __ __ __ __   kind of rabbit

8. __ __ __ __ __ __ __ __ __ __   moving plant

WORD BANK

cactus	desert	hare	lizard
saguaro	tortoise	trailer	tumbleweed

Name_____   **Date**_____

JACK KENT

"The Once-Upon-a-Time Dragon"

Read "The Once-Upon-a-Time Dragon." Use the numbers 1 through 9 to put the story events in order.

_____ Sam breathed fire for the circus manager.

_____ Sam thought he was under a magic spell.

_____ Sam went to bed 87 times a day because he loved bedtime stories.

_____ Sam fed the pigeons with Mr. Johnson.

_____ Mr. Johnson went to the circus to see Sam.

_____ Sam and Mr. Johnson fed the pigeons together.

_____ Sam turned into a man who looked just like Mr. Johnson.

_____ Sam was happy to be himself.

_____ Sam changed back into a dragon.

Name _____   **Date** _____

EZRA JACK KEATS

"Peter's Chair"

Read "Peter's Chair." Use the words in the Word Bank to unscramble the words below.

1. DINGBULI   __ __ __ __ __ __ __ __

2. BRIC   __ __ __ __

3. STIRES   __ __ __ __ __ __

4. SHARC   __ __ __ __ __

5. TAPIN   __ __ __ __ __

6. CRAHI   __ __ __ __ __

7. WODWIN   __ __ __ __ __ __

8. TRAINUC   __ __ __ __ __ __ __

9. KIPN   __ __ __ __

10. SPOHPGIN   __ __ __ __ __ __ __ __

WORD BANK

BUILDING	CHAIR	CRASH	CRIB	CURTAIN
PAINT	PINK	SHOPPING	SISTER	WINDOW

Name_____   **Date**_____

SID FLEISCHMAN

"McBroom's Ghost"

Read "McBroom's Ghost." Use the words in the Word Bank to finish the sentences.

1. The winter was so cold, a match flame would _____.

2. The children thought they heard the _____ crow.

3. Heck Jones was as _____ as his hogs.

4. McBroom heard his own voice in the _____.

5. To scare away ghosts, burn a pile of _____.

6. Heck Jones' hogs ate McBroom's _____.

7. It was so cold, the red barns turned _____.

8. There wasn't a haunt, just _____ thawing after a very cold winter.

WORD BANK

| blue | corn | freeze | mean |
| rooster | shoes | sounds | woodpile |

Name_____ Date_____

MITSUMASA ANNO

"Anno's Alphabet" "Anno's Counting Book"

FOR THE TEACHER

These books are two classics to use with pre-school and Kindergarten children.

Anno's Alphabet

Show the children *Anno's Alphabet*. Let them look through the pages to find the hidden pictures in the border. They begin with the same letter as is in the center of the page. *Demi's Find The Animal ABC* is another good book to use. Find all the alphabet books you can (if you have any by Tony Palazzo— they're terrific, as well as Van Allsburg's *The Z Was Zapped*) and let the children look and talk and share their observations with you and their fellow students.

Have plenty of paper and drawing materials available. Ask them if they would like to make an alphabet by printing, painting, carving in clay, or whatever...

Child's play is child's learning. Let them fall in love with working with letters.

Anno's Counting Book

Share *Anno's Counting Book* with your class. It also offers children an opportunity to work with manipulatives. Give the children the same media materials as with *Anno's Alphabet*. Ask them to make their own counting book. They can draw whatever they like; i.e., one cat, two trucks, three hippos, etc. They will learn to think of numbers in the same positive way as they do letters.

MARGARET MAHY

"The Boy Who Was Followed Home"

Read "The Boy Who Was Followed Home." Answer the questions about the thing that followed you home one day.

1. If you could be followed home by an animal, what would you choose?

_____

2. Where would you keep your new-found pet?

_____

3. What does your pet like to eat? _____ .

4. Does your pet have any strange habits? Name the strange habit.

_____

5. How do your parents feel about the new pet?

_____

_____

6. Use the back of this page to write about one very short adventure you had with your

pet.

Name_____ **Date**_____

HARRY DEVLIN

"Cranberry Mystery"

Read "Cranberry Mystery." Things disappeared all over Cranberryport. See if you can find them in this word search puzzle. Use the words in the Word Bank as your guide.

```
L F P A G X O F M U M I T P B W E
L F A N T I Q U E S X T U C A D Q
D M I R R O R S C R E A F L R S A
O K N G W H X I U L L F E Z I O D
H O T D U Q Z K T O O O P W K S E
S P I S A R A T Y J D C H A I R S
V A N E G I E J H T E M K G U V K
A R G K L K G H O Z P Q T S N A V
P F S Z H H L T E R D V I N W C N
A N K Y R O Z P S A U S H P M P S
C I Q M C S J A A Q D A Y K U V J
```

WORD BANK

antiques	chairs	clocks	desk	figurehead
kettle	mirrors	paintings	vane	

Name _____ **Date** _____

ROBERT FROST

"You Come Too: Favorite Poems for Young Readers"

Read "Mending Wall," "Stopping by Woods on a Snowy Evening," and "The Last Word of the Bluebird" in *You Come Too: Favorite Poems for Young Readers*. Answer the questions about the poems.

A. MENDING WALL:

Mending stone fences is a spring tradition. The writer and his neighbor do it out of habit. But the writer thinks it is silly. Find his two reasons for not needing a wall.

1. _____

2. _____

B. STOPPING BY WOODS ON A SNOWY EVENING:

The writer stops his horse just to enjoy the beauty of snow falling in a wooded area. Can you name two or more things that you think are really beautiful?

1. _____

2. _____

C. LAST WORD OF A BLUEBIRD:

The crow gives the writer a message for Lesley from the bluebird. Fill in the blanks of the message. The clues are in the Word Bank.

Dear Lesley,

The north wind made it ____ ____ ____ ____ last night.

There was ____ ____ ____ on the trough.

It gave me a very bad ____ ____ ____ ____ ____.

Be sure to wear your ____ ____ ____ ____

See you in the ____ ____ ____ ____ ____ ____

Love, Bluebird

WORD BANK				
cold	cough	hood	ice	spring

Name_____ **Date**_____

 **MARCH READERS**

 **BOOKS**
GOLDEN WONDERS!

 **GOOD LUCK!** **BOOKS BRING YOU** **GOOD LUCK!**

MARCH INTO READING

MARCH INTO READING!

WISH FOR GREAT BOOKS

MARCH ANSWER KEY

LEO AND DIANE DILLION: *Why Mosquitoes Buzz in People's Ears*

1. mosquito
2. iguana
3. python
4. rabbit
5. monkey
6. owl
7. lion
8. antelope
9. crow
10. elephant

DR. SEUSS: *Bartholomew and the Oobleck*

1. Didd
2. rain; fog; snow; sunshine
3. magicians
4. Oobleck
5. glue
6. crown
7. sorry
8. chased

THACHER HURD: *Mystery on the Docks*

1. Ralph
2. Eduardo Bombasto was kidnapped
3. On the dock
4. Two rats didn't pay for their dinner. Or: They took a bag out of the car.
5. He wanted a ransom.

EDNA MILLER: *Mousekin Takes a Trip*

1. trailer
2. desert
3. cactus
4. lizard
5. tortoise
6. saguaro
7. hare
8. tumbleweed

JACK KENT: *The Once-Upon-a-Time Dragon*

4, 2, 1, 9, 5, 8, 3, 7, 6

EZRA JACK KEATS: Peter's Chair

1. building
2. crib
3. sister
4. crash
5. paint
6. chair
7. window
8. curtain
9. pink
10. shopping

SID FLEISCHMAN: *McBroom's Ghost*

1. freeze
2. rooster
3. mean
4. woodpile
5. shoes
6. corn
7. blue
8. sounds

HARRY DEVLIN: *Cranberry Mystery*

```
L F P A G X O F M U M I T P B W E
L F A N T I Q U E S X T U C A D Q
D M I R R O R S C R E A F L R S A
O K N G W H X I U L L F E Z I O D
H O T D U Q Z K T O O P W K S E
S P I S A R A T Y J D C H A I R S
V A N E G I E J H T E M K G U V K
A R G K L K G H O Z P Q T S N A V
P F S Z H H L T E R D V I N W C N
A N K Y R O Z P S A U S H P M P S
C I Q M C S J A A Q D A Y K U V J
```

ROBERT FROST: *You Come Too: Favorite Poems for Young Readers*
   A. 1. different trees
      2. just for the sake of tradition
   B. Answers will vary
   C. 1. cold
      2. ice
      3. cough
      4. hood
      5. spring

MARCH AUTHORS BIBLIOGRAPHY

March 1   Lonzo Anderson

Two Hundred Rabbits (Viking, 1968—out of print).

March 2   Leo Dillon

Illustrator with Diane Dillon of: *The Hundred-Penny Box* by Sharon B. Mathias (Viking, 1975); *Why Mosquitoes Buzz in People's Ears*, retold by Verna Aardema (Dial, 1975)—1976 Caldecott Award winner; *Ashanti to Zulu: African Traditions* by Margaret Musgrove (Dial, 1976)—1977 Caldecott Award winner; *Who's in Rabbit's House?*, retold by Verna Aardema (Dial, 1979); *Brother to the Wind* by Mildred P. Walter (Lothrop, 1985); *Honey, I Love: And Other Poems* by Eloise Greenfield (Harper, 1986).

March 2   Dr. Seuss (Theordore Geisel)

McElligot's Pool (Random House, 1947)—1948 Caldecott Honor book; *Bartholemew and the Oobleck* (Random House, 1949)—1950 Caldecott Honor book; *If I Ran the Zoo* (Random House, 1950)—1951 Caldecott Honor book; other eternal favorites, all published by Random House: *Green Eggs and Ham*, *There's a Wocket in My Pocket*, *The Cat in the Hat*, *The Cat in the Hat Comes Back*, *On Beyond Zebra*, etc.

March 6   Thacher Hurd

He's the son of Edith Thacher Hurd and Clement Hurd: *Axle the Freeway Cat* (Harper, 1981); *Hobo Dog* (Scholastic, 1981); *Mystery on the Docks* (Harper, 1983); *Mama Don't Allow* (Harper, 1984); *Hobo Dog in the Ghost Town* (Scholastic, 1986); *Pea Patch Jig* (Crown, 1986); *Hobo Dog's Christmas Tree* (Scholastic, 1986).

March 8   Edna Miller

Cute mouse series published by Prentice Hall: *Mousekin Finds a Friend*, *Mousekin Takes a Trip*, *Mousekin's ABCs*, *Mousekin's Birth*, *Mousekin's Christmas Eve*, *Mousekin's Close Call*, *Mousekin's Fables*, *Mousekin's Family*, *Mousekin's Golden House*, *Mousekin's Mystery*, *Mousekin's Thanksgiving*, *Mousekin's Woodland Sleepers*.

March 9   Joan M. Lexau

I Should Have Stayed in Bed (Harper, 1965); *Rooftop Mystery* (Harper, 1968); *Striped Ice Cream* (Scholastic, 1971); *Emily and the Klunky Baby and the Next-Door Dog* (Dial, 1972); *Poison Ivy Case* (Dial, 1984); *Don't Be My Valentine* (Harper, 1985); *Dog Food Caper* (Dial, 1985); *The Homework Caper* (Harper, 1985); *The Christmas Secret* (Scholastic, 1986).

March 10   Jack Kent

There's No such Thing as a Dragon (Western, 1975); *Jack Kent's Happy-Ever-After Book* (Random, 1976); *Supermarket Magic* (Random, 1978); *Scribble Monster* (HBJ, 1981); *The Once-Upon-a-Time Dragon* (HBJ, 1982); *Silly Goose* (Prentice Hall, 1983).

March 11   Wanda Gag

All published by Putnam: *Snow White and the Seven Dwarfs* (1938)—1939 Caldecott Honor book; *Nothing at All* (1941)—1942 Caldecott Honor book; *The Funny Thing* (1960); *Gone Is Gone* (1960); *Snippy and Snappy* (1960); *Millions of Cats* (1977); *The ABC Bunny* (1978); *The Sorcerer's Apprentice*, with Margot Tomes (1978); *The Earth Gnome* (1985).

March 11   Ezra Jack Keats

The Snowy Day (Viking, 1962)—1963 Caldecott Award winner; *Jennie's Hat* (Harper, 1966); *Goggles* (Macmillan, 1969)—1970 Caldecott Honor book; *Hi, Cat* (Macmillan, 1970); *The Little Drummer Boy* (Macmillan, 1972); *Dreams* (Macmillan, 1974); *Kitten for a Day* (Macmillan, 1974); *A Whistle for Willie* (Penguin, 1977); *The Trip* (Greenwillow, 1978); *Louie's Search* (Macmillan, 1980); *Clementina's Cactus* (Viking, 1982); *Louie* (Greenwillow, 1983); *Peter's Chair* (Harper, 1983); *Apartment Three* (Macmillan, 1986); *Maggie & the Pirate* (Macmillan, 1987); *Pet Show!* (Macmillan, 1987).

March 13   Diane Dillon

She and her husband, Leo Dillon, have illustrated many books. See "March 2, Leo Dillon" for a listing.

March 16   Sid Fleischman

The Whipping Boy (Greenwillow, 1986)—1987 Newbery Award winner; McBroom series for third grade readers published by Little, Brown: *McBroom's Almanac, McBroom's Ghost*, etc.; Bloodhound Gang mystery series for third grade readers published by Random House: *Bloodhound Gang in the Case of the Secret Message,—the 264-Pound Burglar,—Princess Tomorrow,—the Cackling Ghost,—the Flying Clock.*

March 17   Kate Greenaway

New editions of the timeless illustrations of this first great children's illustrator are now available: *Mother Goose: Or the Old Nursery Rhymes* (Warne, 1882); *Mother Goose* (Evergreen, 1973); *The Language of Flowers* (Warne, 1977); *A: Apple Pie* (Warne, 1987).

March 20   Mitsumasa Anno

Topsy-Turvies: Pictures to Stretch the Imagination (Weatherhill, 1970); *Upside-Downers: More Pictures to Stretch the Imagination* (Weatherhill, 1971); *Anno's Alphabet* (Crowell, 1975); *Anno's Counting Book* (Crowell, 1977); *Anno's Ani-*

mals (Putnam: 1979); *Anno's Journey* (Putnam, 1981); *Anno's USA* (Putnam, 1983); *In Shadowland* (Orchard Books, 1988).

March 21   Margaret Mahy

A Lion in the Meadow (Watts, 1969—out of print); *The Dragon of an Ordinary Family* (Watts, 1969—out of print); *The Boy Who Was Followed Home* (Dial, 1983); *Baby's Breakfast* (Children's Press, 1986); *Trouble on the Bus* (Children's Press, 1986); *The Man Whose Mother Was a Pirate* (Viking, 1986); *Jam* (Atlantic Monthly, 1986).

March 21   Phyllis McGinley

The Year Without a Santa Claus (Lippincott, 1957).

March 22   Randolph Caldecott

Some of his best work has been published in three volumes by Warne: *A First Caldecott Collection, A Second Caldecott Collection, A Third Caldecott Collection*; *The Caldecott Aesop: Twenty Fables* (Doubleday, 1978).

March 22   Harry Devlin

Illustrated the Cranberry series written by Wende Devlin and published by Macmillan: *Cranberry Christmas, Cranberry Halloween, Cranberry Mystery, Cranberry Thanksgiving, Cranberry Valentine* (all titles include a recipe to prepare a treat with the children); *Hang on Hester* (Lothrop, 1980); *Old Witch and the Polka-Dot Ribbon* (Macmillan, 1980).

March 23   Eleanor Cameron

Mushroom Planet series for third grade readers published by Little, Brown: *Mr. Bass's Planetoid, Stowaway to the Mushroom Planet, Time and Mr. Bass, The Wonderful Flight to the Mushroom Planet.*

March 26   Robert Frost

A great American poet: *You Come Too: Favorite Poems for Young Readers* (Holt, 1959); *Stopping by Woods on a Snowy Evening* (Dutton, 1978)—this picture book shows why the man stopped at the woods.

March 26   Betty MacDonald

Mrs. Piggle-Wiggle series for end-of-year second graders and beginning third graders published by Lippincott: *Mrs. Piggle-Wiggle's Farm, Mrs. Piggle-Wiggle's Magic.* There are other titles out of print; check the library's shelves.

March 30   Charles Keller

He's the "king of jokes and puns," with his books published by Prentice Hall: *Alexander the Grape; Astronauts: Space Jokes and Riddles; Ballpoint Bananas and Other Jokes for Children; More Ballpoint Bananas; Count Draculation: Monster Riddles; Daffynitions; Giggle Puss: Pet Jokes for Kids; Grime Doesn't Pay; Norma Lee, I Don't Knock on Doors*; etc.

March 31   Beni Montresor

Illustrated *May I Bring a Friend?* by Beatrice DeRegniers (Macmillan, 1964)—1965 Caldecott Award winner; *Bedtime* (Harper, 1978).

APRIL

April 2	Hans Christian Andersen, *The Little Match Girl* (fill in)
April 4	Elizabeth Levy, *Something Queer at the Haunted School* (mystery words)
April 7	Donald Carrick, *Harold and the Giant Knight* (fill in)
April 8	Ruth Chew, *No Such Thing as a Witch* (wordsearch)
April 10	David Adler, *Cam Jansen and the Mystery of the Carnival Prize* (mystery words)
April 12	C. W. Anderson, *Billy and Blaze* (fill in)
April 15	Joy Berry, *What to Do When Mom or Dad Say...* (do something besides watch TV)
April 16	Gertrude Chandler Warner, *The Boxcar Children* (wordsearch)
April 24	Evaline Ness, *Sam, Bangs, and Moonshine* (fill in)
April 26	Patricia Reilly Giff, *The Beast in Miss Rooney's Room* (wordsearch)
April 27	Ludwig Bemelmans, *Madeline's Rescue* (rhyming words)
April 27	John Burningham, *Would You Rather?* (writing activity)
April 27	Wende Devlin, *Cranberry Valentine* ("unvalentine" activity)

April Bookmarks
April Answer Key
April Authors Bibliography

APRIL AUTHORS

DATE	NAME	Author	Illustrator	K	1	2	3
1	Jan Wahl	X	X	X	X		
2	Hans Christian Andersen	X				X	X
3	Washington Irving	X					X
4	Elizabeth Levy	X				X	X
7	Tony Palazzo	X	X	X	X	X	
7	Donald Carrick	X	X			X	X
8	Ruth Chew	X				X	X
8	Trina Schart Hyman		X				
10	David Adler	X				X	X
10	Clare Turlay Newberry	X			X	X	
12	C.W. Anderson	X			X	X	
12	Beverly Cleary	X		X	X	X	
12	Hardie Gramatky	X		X	X	X	
15	Eleanor Schick	X			X	X	
15	Joy Berry	X				X	X
16	Gertrude Chandler Warner	X				X	X
22	Kurt Wiese	X				X	X
24	Evaline Ness	X	X			X	X
25	Alvin Schwartz					X	X
26	Patricia Reilly Giff	X				X	X
27	Wende Devlin	X				X	X
27	Judith Vigna	X				X	X
27	Ludwig Bemelmens	X	X	X	X	X	
27	John Burningham	X	X	X	X		

HANS CHRISTIAN ANDERSEN

"The Little Match Girl"

Read "The Little Match Girl." Use the words in the Word Bank to finish these sentences about a little girl who spends the last evening of the year seeing beautiful visions and going on a new journey with her grandmother. An excellent version of this Andersen tale is published by Houghton Mifflin, 1968 illustrated by Caldecott-winning Blair Lent.

1. It was the _____ evening of the year.

2. A poor _____ girl walked through the streets.

3. No one had bought any of her _____.

4. She had lost her _____.

5. She was very nearly _____.

6. She crouched between two _____.

7. She lit a match to be _____.

8. She saw a great polished _____.

9. In the second match flame she saw a _____.

10. In the third, she saw a _____ _____.

11. A _____ fell out of the sky.

12. Grandmother took the girl above the _____.

WORD BANK

| buildings | Christmas | earth | feast | frozen | last | |
| little | matches | slippers | star | stove | tree | warm |

Name _____ **Date** _____

ELIZABETH LEVY

"Something Queer at the Haunted School"

Read "Something Queer at the Haunted School." Answer the Who, What, Where, How, and Why questions about this mystery.

1. Who stayed late to make Fletcher a costume? _____.

2. Name three strange things that happened at the haunted school.

_____

_____

_____

3. What does Gwen do when she thinks? _____.

4. Where do Gwen and Jill do research? _____.

5. Who did Gwen and Jill visit at his home? _____.

6. What other name was on his mailbox? _____.

7. What did he put on his desk drawer? _____.

8. What haunted building did the girls visit? _____.

9. Who wrote the book about that haunted place? _____.

10. What did they meet on the roof? _____.

11. Who haunted the school? _____.

12. Who had the dream? _____.

Name_____   Date_____

DONALD CARRICK

"Harald and the Giant Knight"

Read "Harald and the Giant Knight." Use the words in the Word Bank to finish these sentences about a brave little boy who scares away the bad knights.

1. Harald and his parents lived in a _____.

2. Harald's father was a _____ and a _____.

3. Harald wanted to be a _____.

4. The knights came to _____ on Harald's _____.

5. They _____ what they wanted.

6. They _____ his father's _____ trees.

7. They acted like _____.

8. Harald and his parents made a _____ knight.

9. Their _____ carried the knight.

10. The knight _____ the other knights away.

11. Harald and his parents finally planted their _____.

12. Part of the giant knight became a _____.

WORD BANK

chopped	crops	farmer	fruit	giant
horse	knight	land	practice	scared
scarecrow	thieves	took	valley	weaver

Name_____ Date_____

RUTH CHEW

"No Such Thing as a Witch"

Read "No Such Thing as a Witch." Find the words from the Word Bank in the word search puzzle below.

Ruth Chew has written many witch stories as wonderful as this one. If you really liked this story, you'll be glad to know there are more.

```
Z U I O E H Z M Z R V R D R I M W M U J
M T N T U V A N O A C M Y S R A D O L Z
J E N A A F U N J K P B P Z K G P I B R
T M M K X T B X K Q Z S X V Y G N V G M
W S V N U F H B N I U V Z G W I N D O W
E P V R N U M G V R E B U T T E R R N I
Y G G W E P P F Z P Y R S Y H M E L N K
I S C N I S T G D T Q D T C U P T Y H F
S M F S G T W O F F D T T L A E T G Q W
N Q N M H A C O Z O F I S P G A N X V B
S T U Z B I O H T N K Y S C H O O L D C
D G I I O R V O B Z O W N H C P Z X V R
M J S M R S C O O P E R T D W E F R E A
E G A P A R T M E N T R A U A A A Y G R
F E N C E U E N I A G F Y R V N S E T M
Z H C H Z M B L E R M J B Q E U Z H N I
L G E W C V O G W Q I W X W J T G V E E
G L R A D J T F P I T O M S I O Y B Q R
```

Word Bank

DISHWASHER	NEWSPAPER	MRSCOOPER	APARTMENT	SQUIRREL
NEIGHBOR	NUISANCE	UPSTAIRS	KITCHEN	PEANUT
BUTTER	SCHOOL	WINDOW	MAGGIE	FENCE
WITCH	ROOF	WAVE	TODD	NORA

Name _____ Date _____

DAVID ADLER

"Cam Jansen and the Mystery of the Carnival Prize"

Read "Cam Jansen and the Mystery of the Carnival Prize." Answer the Who, What, Where, How, and Why questions about this mystery.

1. Who can remember everything she sees? _____.

2. Who kept winning at the coin toss? _____.

3. What was the same about the girl? _____.

4. What was the same about the boy? _____.

5. How did Cam know they were the same? _____.

6. How were the dimes "fixed"? _____

_____

Why? _____

_____

7. What was under the Dime Toss game board? _____.

8. What did Bert and Sylvia do to make up for their cheating?

_____

© 1989 by The Center for Applied Research in Education

Name_____ **Date**_____

C. W. ANDERSON

"Billy and Blaze"

Read "Billy and Blaze." Use the words in the Word Bank to finish these sentences about Billy and his horse Blaze.

1. Billy loved _____ more than anything.

2. He rode on a _____ horse.

3. Billy had a very special _____ present.

4. Billy's present had a _____ nose and feet.

5. Billy called his pony _____.

6. Billy went to the _____ with a _____ to check on Blaze.

7. Blaze liked to eat _____ and _____.

8. They went for a long ride after _____.

9. They found a _____ caught in a _____.

10. Billy put a _____ on the dog's foot.

11. Billy entered a jumping _____.

12. He won a _____ cup.

WORD BANK

bandage	birthday	Blaze	breakfast	carrots
contest	dog	farmer's	flashlight	horses
silver	stable	sugar	trap	white

Name_____ Date_____

JOY BERRY

"Do Something Besides Watch TV"

Read "What To Do When Mom Or Day Says... 'Do Something Besides Watch TV.'" Growing up is sometimes a difficult chore. We have lots of help from parents, friends, relatives, and wonderful authors like Joy Berry.

Joy Berry has a wonderful series of books called "The Survival Series." They teach us how to make good choices about growing up. Some titles help us get along with others. Other titles help us do things that are good for us as a person. This book will help you take care of yourself when you find that you are bored. If we grow up correctly, we will be able to think of good things to do by ourselves when we are bored. We shouldn't always depend on Mom and Dad or others.

Joy's book is filled with good advice. The sign on the back of this sheet will help you remember her important ideas for taking care of your own boredom.

Color the poster.

Find a special place for it in your room. If your parents don't mind, hang it on your door, on your wall, or on your refrigerator. A reminder isn't helpful if you can't see it.

Enjoy your poster and remember "Do something besides watch TV." It turns your brain into guacomole anyway!

WHEN I'M BORED

SHOULD I BE DOING SOMETHING?

DO I WANT TO BE WITH SOMEONE SPECIAL?

WHERE DO I WANT TO BE?

WHAT DO I WANT TO DO?

BY JOY BERRY

GERTRUDE CHANDLER WARNER

"The Boxcar Children"

Read "The Boxcar Children." Find the words from the Word Bank in the word search puzzle below.

The Alden family children love to solve mysteries. If you like this book, you'll be happy to know there are more.

```
Q U R Y V E K O V Z E M U O C Q D D H H
Z O P P I L L O W S Z H T J E C N M U T
W I O S O B A K E R Y A T F H D T Z V O
E M S S L F W U U Y R O D H H M M C I V
V E J Q E Y A K N J B J H W K W O J F R
J A K F T O K N K D O E U F W H E N R Y
D N I K X K E A A G R A N D F A T H E R
P N Y Y K B D E A A X Y G C L X R I H Y
K M J D K X R B P C A R R Y H P D X V D
O A M P B B O N B X J M Y R X E T C Q Y
T S O C A I V V O F G Y K S R V S J G D
Q R S V X X L Y G X P L W I R P B O I T
V T K V U X A H V J O B T S B Y V G I E
```

Word Bank

GRANDFATHER	LAUNDRY	PILLOWS
BENCHES	HUNGRY	BAKERY
VIOLET	JESSIE	BREAD
AWAKE	CARRY	MONEY
KNIFE	TIRED	HENRY
BENNY	MEAN	BAG

Name_____ Date_____

EVALINE NESS

"Sam, Bangs, and Moonshine"

Read "Sam, Bangs, and Moonshine." Use the words in the Word Bank to finish these sentences about a little girl who learns the truth about "moonshine." Evaline Ness wrote and illustrated this 1967 Caldecott Medal Winner.

1. Sam lived near a large _____.

2. Sam loved to make up strange _____.

3. Her mother was a _____.

4. She had a _____ in her house.

5. Her _____ was pulled by _____.

6. _____ believed everything Sam said.

7. Sam's kangaroo was never at _____.

8. Sam sent Thomas to a cave on Blue _____.

9. Bangs was washed away in the _____.

10. But he came back to her _____.

11. Sam's dad gave her a _____.

12. Sam called the little animal _____.

WORD BANK

chariot	dragons	gerbil	harbor
home	kangaroo	mermaid	Moonshine
Rock	stories	storm	Thomas	window

Name _____ Date _____

PATRICIA REILLY GIFF

The Beast in Miss Rooney's Room
Richard's Beastly Words

Read *The Beast in Miss Rooney's Room*. Find the beastly words from the Word Bank in the word search puzzle below.

```
J C D C G J N L Z H H U T W N U L
K P N N S I L Y H I N H O L L Y U
C R G Z F A Q B L U P R U Q J B D
C V I G Z S T A G E R P G M X Q B
H H K P N R L N K A F N H D V B S
P F V T U F B D N P I C T U R E S
H B X U R P J A X L S R M X F R B
B T O B S F P G L R H D P J Y Y X
K G J O E I S E U Q B R H L L U S
E O N Q K R P H T I O A I L A G Y
B A B I E S U G S S W W N W D N A
B S W J C T N L J D L N S N R J E
M I I I G I I E H I Q E U G E D L
V S E G D F C F A G T L T T S R M
L T Y A C U O T Z K T Q S C P A N
Z E E O V M R B C V E Z I E W M D
A R T I S T N A Z T E R P P R Q T
H F G G M J O C R G T C S B G M Z
I S Z A Y Q P K G Q H I W D W V W
```

Word Bank

FISHBOWL	AIRPLANE	SPELLING	SNEAKERS	PICTURES
LEFTBACK	BANDAGE	UNICORN	PUPPETS	READING
ARTIST	SISTER	BABIES	BANNER	FIRST
STAGE	ARROW	NURSE	HOLLY	TOUGH
BOOKS	TEETH	DRAW		

Name_____   Date_____

LUDWIG BEMELMANS

"Madeline's Rescue"

Read "Madeline's Rescue." Use the words in the Word Bank to finish these rhyming pairs about this 1954 Caldecott Award Winner.

1. A house covered with vines, was home to girls who walked in two straight _____.

2. Madeline loved snow and ice, and wasn't afraid of _____.

3. Madeline scared Miss Clavell, especially the day she _____.

4. She would have been as dead as a log, except for the bravery of a wonderful _____.

5. They wrapped Madeline's head, and put her right to _____.

6. There was a _____ over who'd sleep with doggie that night.

7. An old lady came. "What's this dog? Who's to _____?"

8. She made the dog leave. Poor, poor, _____.

9. They looked high and low, and anywhere a dog might _____.

10. In the middle of the _____, she sat by the street _____.

11. Wagging her tail with all her _____.

12. There was another fight over the _____.

13. Soon there were enough puppies to go _____!

WORD BANK							
around	bed	blame	dog	fell	fight	Genevieve	
go	hound	light	lines	mice	might	night	right

Name_____ **Date**_____

© 1989 by The Center for Applied Research in Education

JOHN BURNINGHAM

"Would You Rather?"

Read "Would You Rather …?" This is an excellent chance for us to be creative! John Burningham has given us a good start on thinking about strange and unusual events. Let's continue.

Use the lines below to create new situations to make decisions about. You can write situations for

eating…
walking in…
riding on…
sleeping on…
being visited by a…
see…in your bed
things your brother or sister do to your room, clothes, homework
things you'd see in school, at the zoo, in the park, driving down the street
or WHAT ELSE?

Read the example and then Write Your Own on plain white paper. Draw pictures to go along with your writing.

Would you rather eat…
    puny pickled peppers

    french fried bunny feet

    cinnamon slugs

    ice cream with spider sauce
         or

    hot fudge mushrooms!

Name_____   **Date**_____

WENDE DEVLIN

"Cranberry Valentine"

Read "Cranberry Valentine." Even though it isn't Valentine's Day, we can still send an "UnValentine" card to a special person. It will be a special way to say...

I LOVE YOU!!

Read the examples:

I know it isn't Valentine's Day!
But I want to say—
I Love You ANYWAY
On our special UnValentine Day.

Valentine's day isn't here,
It's UnValentine's Day, ain't it queer.
I'm too early I fear.
But since you're near
I want you to hear,
I love you, sweetie dear!

I could be early,
Or I could be late.
But I couldn't wait
To say you're great
Happy UnValentine's Day
In my special way.

Practice your verse on the lines below. Write it on clean paper when it's perfect. Decorate your UnValentine and give it to someone you love!

_____

_____

_____

_____

Name_____ **Date**_____

APRIL READERS

APRIL SHOWERS

BRING READING TIME

LIBRARY CLOSED

APRIL FOOL!

WATCH OUT!

IT'S APRIL FOOL'S DAY

HAPPY EASTER

HAPPY EASTER

APRIL ANSWER KEY

HANS CHRISTIAN ANDERSON: *The Little Match Girl*

1. last
2. little
3. matches
4. slippers
5. frozen
6. buildings
7. warm
8. stove
9. feast
10. Christmas Tree
11. star
12. earth

ELIZABETH LEVY: *Something Queer at the Haunted House*

1. Jill and Gwen
2. (a) They heard a scream; (b) glowing lights appeared on the stage during a play; (c) weird noises were heard on the PA system; (d) all flags were turned upside-down; (e) saw strange writing on the chalkboard.
3. Taps her braces
4. School library
5. Mr. Murdoch
6. Ross
7. Plans for a dream house
8. Laundromat
9. Veronica Ross/Mr. Murdock
10. A werewolf
11. Mr. Murdoch
12. Flectcher

DONALD CARRICK: *Harald and the Giant Knight*

1. valley
2. farmer, weaver
3. knight
4. practice, land
5. took
6. chopped, fruit
7. thieves
8. giant
9. horse
10. scared
11. crops
12. scarecrow

April Answer Key

RUTH CHEW: *No Such Thing as a Witch*

```
Z U I O E H Z M Z R V R D R I M W M U J
M T N T U V A N O A C M Y S R A D O L Z
J E N A A F U N J K P B P Z K G P I B R
T M M K X T B X K Q Z S X V Y G N V G M
W S V N U F H B N I U V Z G W I N D O W
E P V R N U M G V R E B U T T E R R N I
Y G G W E P P F Z P Y R S Y H M E L N K
I S C N I S T G D T Q D T C U P T Y H F
S M F S G T W O F D T T L A E T G Q W
N Q N M H A C Z O F I S P G A N X V B
S T U Z B I H T N K Y S C H O O L D C
D G I I O R V O B Z W N H C P Z X V R
M J S M R S C O O P E R T D W E F R E A
E G A P A R T M E N T R A U A A A Y G R
F E N C E U N I A G F Y R V N S E T M
Z H C H Z M B L E R M J B Q E U Z H N I
L G E W C V O G W Q I W X W J T G V E E
G L R A D J T F P I T O M S I O Y B Q R
```

DAVID ADLER: *Cam Jansen & the Mystery of the Carnival Prize*

1. Cam Jansen
2. A boy and a girl
3. Braces
4. Curly blond hair
5. Her "mental camera" remembered braces and blond curly hair.
6. With aluminum foil and a slug
7. So they would stop in the winning circle
8. A magnet
9. Put away library books

C. W. ANDERSON: *Billy & Blaze*

1. horses
2. farmer's
3. birthday
4. white
5. Blaze
6. stable; flashlight
7. carrots; sugar
8. breakfast
9. dog; trap
10. bandage
11. contest
12. silver

GERTRUDE CHANDLER WARNER: *The Boxcar Children*

```
Q U R Y V E K O V Z E M U O C Q D D H H
Z O P P I L L O W S Z H T J E C N M U T
W I O S O B A K E R Y A T F H D T Z V O
E M S S L F W U U Y R O D H H M M C I V
V E J Q E Y A K N J B J H W K W O J F R
J A K F T O K N K D O E U F W H E N R Y
D N I K X K E A A G R A N D F A T H E R
P N Y Y K B D E A A X Y G C L X R I H Y
K M J D K X R B P C A R R Y H P D X V D
O A M P B B O N B X J M Y R X E T C Q Y
T S O C A I V V O F G Y K S R V S J G D
Q R S V X X L Y G X P L W I R P B O I T
V T K V U X A H V J O B T S B Y V G I E
```

EVALINE NESS: *Sam, Bangs, & Moonshine*

1. harbor
2. stories
3. mermaid
4. kangaroo
5. chariot; dragons
6. Thomas
7. home
8. Rock
9. storm
10. window
11. gerbil
12. Moonshine

PATRICIA REILLY GIFF: *The Beast in Miss Rooney's Room*

```
J C D C G J N L Z H H U T W N U L
K P N N S I L Y H I N H O L L Y U
C R G Z F A Q B L U P R U Q J B D
C V I G Z S T A G E R P G M X Q B
H H K P N R L N K A F N H D V B S
P F V T U F B D N P I C T U R E S
H B X U R P J A X L S R M X F R B
B T O B S F P G L R H D P J Y Y X
K G J O E I S E U Q B R H L L U S
E O N Q R P H T I O A I L A G Y
B A B I E S U G S S W W N W D N A
B S W J C T N L J D L N S N R J E
M I I I G I T E H I Q E U G E D L
V S E G D F C F A G T L T T S R M
L T Y A C U O T Z Q S C P A N D
Z E E O V M R B C V E Z I E W M D
A R T I S T N A Z T E R P P R Q T
H F G G M J O C R G T C S B G M Z
I S Z A Y Q P K G Q H I W D W V W
```

April Answer Key

LUDWIG BEMELMANS: *Madeline's Rescue*

1. lines
2. mice
3. fell
4. dog
5. bed
6. fight
7. blame

8. Genevieve
9. go
10. night; light
11. might
12. hound
13. around

APRIL AUTHORS BIBLIOGRAPHY

April 1   Jan Wahl

Grandmother Told Me (Little, Brown, 1972—out of print); *Doctor Rabbit's Foundling* (Pantheon, 1977); *Dracula's Cat* (Prentice Hall, 1981); *Tiger Watch* (HBJ, 1982); *Rabbits on Rollerskates* (Crown, 1986); *The Toy Circus* (HBJ, 1986); *Humphrey's Bear* (Holt, 1987).

April 2   Hans Christian Andersen

Current-day authors and illustrators present Hans at his best: *Beauty and the Beast* (Macmillan, 1978); *Thumbelina* (Dial, 1979); *Wild Swans (Dial, 1981); Michael Hague's Favorite Hans Christian Andersen Fairy Tales* (Holt, 1981); *The Emperor's New Clothes*, retold and illustrated by Anne Rockwell (Harper, 1982); *The Snow Queen* (Holt, 1987); other titles to look for in the card catalog or in Andersen collected works: *The Fir Tree, Little Klaus and Big Klaus, The Little Mermaid, The Nightingale, The Red Shoes, The Steadfast Tin Solder, The Ugly Ducklings, The Wild Swans.*

April 3   Washington Irving

Two Tales: Rip Van Winkle & the Legend of Sleepy Hollow (HBJ, 1986).

April 4   Elizabeth Levy

Lizzie Lies a Lot (Dell, 1977); *Something Queer on Vacation* (Delacorte, 1980); *Frankenstein Moved In on the Fourth Floor* (Harper, 1981); *Something Queer Is Going On* (Dell, 1982); *Something Queer at the Haunted School* (Dell, 1983); *Something Queer at the Lemonade Stand* (Dell, 1983); *Something Queer at the Ballpark* (Dell, 1984); *Something Queer at the Library* (Dell, 1984); *Something Queer in Rock 'n Roll* (Delacorte, 1987).

April 7   Tony Palazzo

Timothy Turtle (Scott Foresman, 1946)—1947 Caldecott Honor book; *Animal Family Album* (Lion Books, 1967); *Magic Crayon* (Lion Books, 1967); *Animals of the Night* (Lion Books, 1970); *The Biggest and Littlest Animals* (Lion Books, 1973).

April 7   Donald Carrick

Illustrated Carol Carrick's books published by Houghton Mifflin/Clarion: *Old Mother Witch* (1975); *The Accident* (1976); *The Empty Squirrel* (1981); *Ben & the Porcupine* (1985); *Patrick's Dinosaurs* (1985); illustrated his own titles: *Harald and the Giant Knight* (Houghton Mifflin, 1982); *Milk* (Greenwillow, 1985); *Morgan and the Artist* (Houghton Mifflin, 1985); *Harald and the Great Stag* (Clarion, 1988).

April Authors Bibliography

April 8 Ruth Chew

Enjoyable easy reading Witch series for grades 2-3, newly reprinted by Scholastic: *The Magic Coin, Magic in the Park, Mostly Magic, No Such Thing as a Witch, Secondhand Magic, Summer Magic, The Trouble with Magic, What the Witch Left, The Witch at the Window, The Would-Be Witch.*

April 8 Trina Schart Hyman

Illustrated *Saint George and the Dragon*, retold by Margaret Hodges (Little, Brown, 1984)—1985 Caldecott Award winner; retold and illustrated Grimm's tales: *Little Red Riding Hood, The Sleeping Beauty, Rapunzel,* and others.

April 10 David A. Adler

Cam Jansen series published by Viking: *Cam Jansen and the Mystery at the Monkey House, Mystery Monster Movie, Babe Ruth Baseball, Carnival Prize, Circus Clown, Dinosaur Bones, Gold Coins, Stolen Corn Popper, Stolen Diamonds;* just a bit more difficult for third graders, the Fourth Floor Twins series is published by Viking/Penguin: *Fish Snitch Mystery, Fortune Cookie Chase, Silver Ghost Express;* Jeffrey's Ghost series published by Holt: *Jeffrey's Ghost and the Fifth Grade Dragon, Jeffrey's Ghost and the Ziffel Fair Mystery.*

April 10 Clare Turlay Newberry

Barkis (Harper, 1938)—1939 Caldecott Honor book; *April's Kittens* (Harper, 1940)—1941 Caldecott Honor book.

April 12 C. W. Anderson

Excellent Billy and Blaze series for end-of-year first graders published by Macmillan: *Blaze and the Forest Fire, Blaze and the Gray-Spotted Pony, Blaze and the Indian Cave, Blaze and the Mountain Lion.*

April 12 Beverly Cleary

Among her many, many titles are: *Two Dog Biscuits* (Dell, 1987); *The Growing-Up Feet* (Morrow, 1987); *Janet's Thingamajigs* (Morrow, 1987); *The Real Hole* (Dell, 1987).

April 12 Hardie Gramatky

Little Toot (Putnam, 1959); *Little Toot on the Thames* (Putnam, 1964).

April 15 Joy Berry

Behavior series for grades 2-3 published by Children's Press: *What to Do When Mom and Dad Says...Be Good,—Go to Bed,—Do Something Besides Watch TV,* etc.; Let's Talk About series for grades K-1 published by Children's Press: *Let's Talk About Being Lazy,—Being Destructive,—Tattling—Snooping,* etc.

April Authors Bibliography

April 15   Eleanor Schick

Home Alone (Dial, 1980); *Rainy Sunday* (Dial, 1981); *Joey on His Own* (Dial, 1982); *My Album* (Greenwillow, 1984); *A Piano for Julie* (Greenwillow, 1984); *Art Lessons* (Greenwillow, 1987).

April 16   Gertrude Chandler Warner

The Boxcar Children series for grades 2-3, Alden Family mysteries, published by Albert Whitman: *Benny Uncovers a Mystery, Bicycle Mystery, Blue Bay Mystery, Bus Station Mystery, Houseboat Mystery, Lighthouse Mystery*, etc.

April 22   Kurt Wiese

Fish in the Air (1949 Caldecott Honor book—out of print).

April 24   Evaline Ness

A Pocketful of Cricket (1965 Caldecott Honor book—out of print; *Sam, Bangs, and Moonshine* (Holt, 1966)—1967 Caldecott Award winner.

April 25   Sam Schultz

Joke King series published by Lerner Publications: *101 Animal Jokes, 101 Family Jokes, 101 Knock-Knock Jokes, 101 Monster Jokes, 101 School Jokes.*

April 25   Alvin Schwartz

Published by Harper, these are great for reading out loud to children. Humor selections: *Busy Buzzing Bumblebees* (1982), *All Our Noses Are Here & Other Noodle Tales* (1985), *In a Dark, Dark Room* (1985), and more; tall tales and superstitions: *Witcracks: Jokes and Jests from American Folklore* (1973), *Cross Your Fingers & Spit in Your Hat* (1974), *Whoppers: Tall Tales & Other Lies* (1975).

April 26   Patricia Reilly Giff

Excellent series for second grade readers: The Kids of the Polk Street School: *Today Was a Terrible Day* (Penguin, 1984); *The Almost Awful Play* (Penguin, 1985); *Watch Out, Ronald Morgan* (Penguin, 1986); *Happy Birthday, Ronald Morgan* (Viking, 1986).

April 27   Ludwig Bemelmans

Wrote the Madeline series: *Madeline* (Penguin, 1977)—1940 Caldecott Honor book; *Madeline's Rescue* (Viking, 1953)—1954 Caldecott Award book; *Madeline in London* (Penguin, 1977); *Madeline's Christmas* (Viking, 1985).

April 27   John Burningham

Simple yet elegant stories with marvelous pictures: *Mr. Gumpy's Outing* (Holt, 1971); *Mr. Gumpy's Motor Car* (Crowell, 1976); *Would You Rather?* (Crowell, 1978); *Grandpa* (Crown, 1985); *John Burningham's Colors* (Crown, 1986); *John Burningham's Opposites* (Crown, 1986); *John Burningham's 123* (Crown, 1986).

April 27   Wende Devlin

See "March 22, Harry Devlin" for a listing.

April 27   Judith Vigna

Concept books for difficult topics, all published by Albert Whitman: *The Little Boy Who Loved Dirt & Almost Became a Superslob* (1975); *The Hiding House* (1979); *She's Not My Real Mother* (1980); *Daddy's New Baby* (1982); *Grandma Without Me* (1984); *Nobody Wants a Nuclear War* (1986); *Mommy and Me by Ourselves Again* (1987).

MAY

May 4	Don Wood, *The Napping House* (writing activity)
	Don Wood, *King Bidgood's in the Bathtub* (looking for details)
May 5	Leo Lionni, *Frederick* (poem writing activity)
May 6	Judy Delton, *Brimhall Turns Detective* (mystery words)
May 7	Nonny Hogrogian, *One Fine Day* (fill-in)
May 12	Edward Lear, *Nonsense Poems* (writing activity)
May 18	Lillian Hoban, *Arthur's Prize Reader* (word search)
May 20	Carol Carrick, *Patrick's Dinosaurs* (writing activity)
May 22	Arnold Lobel, *Owl at Home* (word meanings)
May 23	Margaret Wise Brown, *The Runaway Bunny* (changes)
May 23	Peter Parnall, *The Mountain* (word search)
May 25	Martha Alexander, *I'll Protect You from the Jungle Beasts* (word meanings)
May 31	Jay Williams, *Everyone Knows What a Dragon Looks Like* (drawing activity)

May Bookmarks
May Answer Key
May Authors Bibliography

MAY AUTHORS

DATE	NAME	AUTHOR/ILLUSTRATOR		READING LEVEL			
				K	1	2	3
4	Don Wood		X	X	X	X	
5	Leo Lionni	X	X	X	X	X	
6	Judy Delton	X				X	X
6	Giulio Maestro	X	X			X	X
7	Nonny Hogrogian	X	X	X	X	X	X
9	James Barrie	X					X
9	Eleanor Estes	X					X
12	Edward Lear	X	X			X	X
14	George Selden	X				X	X
15	L. Frank Baum	X					X
15	Ellen MacGregor	X					X
18	Lillian Hoban	X	X	X	X	X	
19	Thomas Feelings		X				
20	Carol Carrick	X				X	X
22	Arnold Lobel	X	X	X	X	X	X
23	Margaret Wise Brown	X		X	X	X	
23	Oliver Butterworth	X					X
23	Peter Parnall	X					X
25	Martha Alexander	X	X	X	X	X	
25	Bennett Cerf	X			X	X	
30	Millicent Selsam	X			X	X	X
31	Jay Williams	X					X
31	Elizabeth Coatsworth	X					X

DON WOOD

"The Napping House"

Read "The Napping House." In this delightful story, Audrey and Don pile people and animals higher and higher. It's a cumulative story. Cumulative means that each new part or detail is added to the ones that come before it. If you could pile things up in a balancing act, what would you choose? Let's write a story too.

1. Audrey and Don picked a bedroom. You could pick another room in a house. Would it be the dining room, the play room, or ???

2. Audrey and Don piled up people and animals. What are you going to pile up? Make a short list:

   _____   _____

   _____   _____

   _____   _____

   _____   _____

3. Audrey and Don's story starts very soft and sleepy. It ends with a crash! Will your story be soft and quiet at the beginning too? Will it end with a crash?

4. Don drew the pictures. Can you draw pictures for your story too?

Name _____   **Date** _____

DON WOOD

"King Bidgood's in the Bathtub"

Read "King Bidgood's in the Bathtub." This Caldecott Honor Book is an excellent example of how well pictures can add to a story. Study the pictures and look for all the wonderful details Don put in them.

1. When the knight battles with the King, what other activities do you see?

_____

_____

2. When the Queen dined with the King, what kinds of food did they have? Were there special decorations?

_____

_____

3. When the Duke went fishing with the King, what kinds of animals appeared in and around the tub?

_____

_____

4. What kinds of masks did the court people wear to the King's Bathtub Ball?

_____

_____

Name_____ **Date**_____

LEO LIONNI

"Frederick"

Read "Frederick." Lionni lets us all know that some people (and mice) do special work. Just like him—they save memories in stories. Frederick's poem keeps his family going when the supplies are low.

Let's write a poem like Frederick did. You can write about mice or spring or spring-time mice. Help me finish this one. Then write your own. Remember: the missing words RHYME!

Springtime Mice

In the spring it's nice,

to have friends that are _____.

It's the sunlight we crave,

as we jump and scoot from our _____.

We shake off our winter dust,

and leap and squeak "To the hilltop or _____."

The clover is ready and in purple bloom,

"Move over. I'm hungry. Give me some _____."

Yes, it's nice to be a mouse in the spring.

I can't think of a lovelier _____.

WORD BANK				
bust	cave	mice	room	thing

NOW WRITE ANOTHER ON A CLEAN PIECE OF PAPER!

Name_____ Date_____

JUDY DELTON

"Brimhall Turns Detective"

Read "Brimhall Turns Detective." Answer the Who, What, How, and Why questions about this mystery.

1. Where were the giant footprints? _____.

2. Who saw the giant footprints? _____.

3. What did he think it was? _____.

4. What did he decide to do? _____.

5. Who set off the trap? _____.

6. What did Bear bake? _____.

7. What did Brimhall do when the big hole trap didn't work?

    _____.

8. Who solved the mystery first? _____.

9. What did he see? _____.

10. Who was the "monster"? _____.

11. Who fell in the big hole trap? _____.

12. Who did Brimhall plan to trick? _____.

Name_____ **Date**_____

NONNY HOGROGIAN

"One Fine Day"

_____

Read "One Fine Day." Use the words in the Word Bank to finish these sentences about a poor fox who lost his tail all over a drink of fine milk.

1. A traveling fox is a _____ fox.

2. He'll drink milk, even from a _____.

3. A nasty woman cut off his _____.

4. He asked the cow for milk. The cow needed _____.

5. The field had it, but it needed _____.

6. The stream had it, but fox needed a _____ .

7. The maiden had it, but she wanted a blue _____.

8. The peddler had it, but he wanted an _____.

9. The chicken had it, but she wanted some _____.

10. The miller had it, and he felt _____ for fox.

11. Finally, fox got his tail _____ on.

12. Everyone got what they wanted and we had a great _____!

WORD BANK					
bead	egg	grain	grass	jug	pail
sewed	sorry	story	tail	thirsty	water

Name _____   **Date** _____

© 1989 by The Center for Applied Research in Education

EDWARD LEAR

"The Complete Nonsense Book"

Read several alphabet rhymes from Edward Lear's nonsense collections. Pay attention to the beat and the rhyme. Here are some poems I wrote with several of my little friends.

> R is for the irksome rat
> who didn't have a Sunday hat
> So he traveled to Brittany town
> and bought himself a ruby crown.

> S is for the slithery snake
> Who didn't like my turnip cake.
> So I sent him to the lake
> to gather seaweed with a rake.

You can make an alphabet collection too, if you follow these steps with the form on the next page.

1. Pick a letter of the alphabet and something that begins with that letter, like Q and queen.
2. Place the letter in the box on line 1.
3. Think of words that describe that thing, like lean and mean.
4. Write your first line, like Q IS FOR THE LEAN, MEAN QUEEN.
5. Now it is time to stop and think of words that rhyme with Queen, like bean, dean, green, machine, seen, teen. We stop to think because that is the writer's first job. Think, then write.
6. Your nonsense verse needs to rhyme. You can rhyme the first two lines and the last two lines, or all four lines.

The important idea is to make the poem *show* a picture to the reader's mind. It will make it easy for you to put a picture in the frame on the next page too. Read this example:

Q is for the lean, mean queen
who lunches on a single green bean.
And then she rides to see what can be seen
On her clinking clanking washing machine.

OR YOU CAN RHYME THE FIRST AND LAST TWO LINES, LIKE THIS:

Q is for the tall, lean queen,
who loves to ride her washing machine.
She travels through valley and hill,
Collecting marigolds and dill!

Write your own nonsense verse and draw a picture in the frame to go with it.

Name _____ Date _____

EDWARD LEAR

"Write a Nonsense Poem"

is for _____

_____

_____

_____

Name_____ **Date**_____

LILLIAN HOBAN

"Arthur's Prize Reader"

Read "Arthur's Prize Reader." Find the words from the Word Bank in the word search puzzle below.

```
R D C H A R D S T M K I U V E
X F V V S K I N M L F V H H Y
I P B D U K N O C K S I P O S
M U H S Z E N W J W A K Z N N
H R M O V I E S M D K Q T P Z
O S W D Z C R F P W O H P V W
B E W A R E V G D O O R S L P
B O O K S C S P A P E R Y T H
Y E V J R R A I N C O A T S K
L D A S X E L C C O N T E S T
C I B W B A E T I M U D T I N
E R N X H M S U N I N P G S F
Z F C Z E C M R G C Z T O T V
T F I V L R A E Q S N G T U U
C G G Z P E N C I L U Z K V B
Z X Y D Q A X Z I K W Y V S B
I B C O L D H K L H B H Z R G
C F G G A K J P Q C K K H R S
```

WORD BANK					
beware	books	cold	comics	contest	dancing
dinner	dog	door	hard	help	hobby
ice cream	knock	movies	mud	paper	pencil
picture	purse	rain	raincoat	read	salesman
snow	soda				

Name_____   Date_____

CAROL CARRICK

"Patrick's Dinosaurs"

Read "Patrick's Dinosaurs." Not everyone is lucky enough to be followed around by dinosaurs. But you can have special friends that only you can see. Answer these questions to get ready to write a story about the animal parade that followed you.

1. What followed you around town? Was it a troop of different birds, dogs, cats, or wild animals of all sorts?

   _____

   _____

2. What did you like about the parade that followed you?

   _____

   _____

3. What didn't you like about the animals that followed you?

   _____

   _____

4. Which was your favorite?

   _____

5. Which one did you like the least, or not at all?

   _____

Now you are ready to start your story. Use a clean piece of paper.

Name _____ **Date** _____

ARNOLD LOBEL

"Owl At Home"

Read "Owl At Home." Match the words in the Word Bank to their meanings below.

1. ___ ___ ___   big night bird

2. ___ ___ ___ ___ ___ ___   night meal

3. ___ ___ ___ ___ ___   visitor

4. ___ ___ ___ ___ ___ ___   something to write with

5. ___ ___ ___ ___ ___   cook with this

6. ___ ___ ___   drink from this

7. ___ ___ ___ ___ ___ ___ ___   where you sleep

8. ___ ___ ___ ___ ___ ___   climb these

9. ___ ___ ___ ___ ___ ___   not up, not down

10. ___ ___ ___ ___ ___   moving part of the sea

11. ___ ___ ___ ___   in the night sky

12. ___ ___ ___ ___ ___ ___   headrest in your bed

WORD BANK					
bedroom	cup	guest	middle	moon	owl
pencil	pillow	stairs	stove	supper	waves

Name_____   **Date**_____

MARGARET WISE BROWN

"The Runaway Bunny"

Read "The Runaway Bunny." There are so many things you can be if you want to run away. But there's always something a mother can be to catch you. Use your imagination to answer what your mother would become if you turned into the things below. There are no right or wrong answers here. Have FUN!

What would your mother become, if you turned into a...

1. baseball _____

2. rain cloud _____

3. bee _____

4. grapes _____

5. acorn _____

6. book _____

7. lion _____

8. ant _____

9. car _____

10. horse _____

Name_____   **Date**_____

PETER PARNALL

"The Mountain"

Read "The Mountain." Peter Parnall is concerned with keeping nature beautiful. Sometimes people change nature by leaving trash and litter where it shouldn't be. The next time you go to the woods, park, or playground area—remember the story's ending. Find the words from the Word Bank in the word search puzzle below.

```
A C Z H B P Q U O A A E G U B E E I C
Z I D J O W S F Q A H W A U G O U L A
U K T L R J X L I T T E R L G O U K N
D D I J F W T V N D D H B O T T L E S
B I R D S J O Z B W W O A F F V H R G
J W O U T M D M R X P S G O Y M D K S
W K A B R J Y P S W A T E R F A L L D
D R D S E F H D E E R C Y E S C M E W
M W L K A L S J U N K Z V S H P X Z Y
E Y B I M O U N T A I N X T R A S H K
I C T P D W B P I C N I C Z I P G L A
R U S M P E O P L E G U I N T E W U G
F Q C X J R X P P H L N I H S R N D S
U M O L E S E C E B O H M W D A D B I
S D Q K X H S K K M T Z Y Y A R R E I
```

WORD BANK

birds	bottles	boxes	cans	deer	flowers	forest
garbage	junk	litter	moles	mountain	paper	
parking lot		people	picnic	road	stream	
trash	waterfall					

Name _____   Date _____

MARTHA ALEXANDER

"I'll Protect You from the Jungle Beasts"

Read "I'll Protect You from the Jungle Beasts." Match the words from the Word Bank to their definitions below.

1. ___ ___ ___ ___ ___ ___   wild animals

2. ___ ___ ___ ___   animal with mane

3. ___ ___ ___ ___ ___ ___ ___ ___   animal with a trunk

4. ___ ___ ___ ___ ___   wiggly animal

5. ___ ___ ___ ___ ___   laughing animal

6. ___ ___ ___ ___   small pieces

7. ___ ___ ___ ___   way through forest

8. ___ ___ ___ ___ ___ ___ ___ ___   very, very big

9. ___ ___ ___ ___ ___   high temperature

10. ___ ___ ___ ___   not strong

11. ___ ___ ___ ___   place to live

12. ___ ___ ___   place to sleep

WORD BANK

| beasts | bed | bits | elephant | enormous | fever |
| house | hyena | lion | path | snake | weak |

Name_____   Date_____

JAY WILLIAMS

"Everyone Knows What a Dragon Looks Like"

Read "Everyone Knows What a Dragon Looks Like." Everyone thought they did until a little, old, bald fat man came to the city of Wu. Now that you know what a dragon looks like, draw a picture of a dragon. Your dragon will be different and special. Follow these directions.

1. Draw your dragon in the frame below.
2. Write four to six sentences that describe it in words on the lines below the frame. What special powers does your dragon have. How does it use them?
3. When everyone does this sheet, your class will have a dragon catalog listing many different kinds of dragons.

_____

_____

_____

_____

_____

Name_____ **Date**_____

MAY READERS

WE LOVE OUR MOMS,

FLOWERS ARE NICE,

BUT BOOKS ARE FOREVER

A BOOK BY ANY NAME

IS JUST AS TERRIFIC!

REMEMBER ALL YOUR

FREEDOMS!

ARBOR DAY

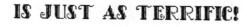

DON WOOD: *King Bidgood's in the Bathtub*

Answers may vary, but some possibilities are:

1. Soldiers pulling cannon, ships sinking, castle towers over tub, knight
2. Cake top is king in tub, court figures on cake, fruit, bread
3. worms, snails, turtles, frog
4. swan, ship, fish, flower, clown

LEO LIONNI: *Frederick*

mice; cave; bust; room; thing

JUDY DELTON: *Brimhall Turns Detective*

1. in the snow
2. Brimhall
3. a monster
4. catch the monster
5. cousin bear
6. cakes
7. sit up all night and wait to see the monster
8. cousin bear
9. Roger's snowshoes and the tracks
10. Roger
11. Brimhall
12. raccoon

NONNY HOGROGIAN: *One Fine Day*

1. thirsty
2. pail
3. tail
4. grass
5. water
6. jug
7. bead
8. egg
9. grain
10. sorry
11. sewed
12. story

LILLIAN HOBAN: *Arthur's Prize Reader*

```
R D C H A R D S T M K I U V E
X F V V S K I N M L F V H H Y
I P B D U K N O C K S I P O S
M U H S Z E N W J W A K Z N N
H R M O V I E S M D K Q T P Z
O S W D Z C R F P W O H P V W
B E W A R E V G D O O R S L P
B O O K S C S P A P E R Y T H
Y E V J R A I N C O A T S K
L D A S X E L C C O N T E S T
C I B W B A E T I M U D T I N
E R N X H M S U N I N P G S F
Z F C Z E C M R G C Z T O T V
T F I V L R A E Q S N G T U U
C G G Z P E N C I L U Z K V B
Z X Y D Q A X Z I K W Y V S B
I B C O L D H K L H B H Z R G
C F G G A K J P Q C K K H R S
```

ARNOLD LOBEL: *Owl at Home*

1. owl
2. supper
3. guest
4. pencil
5. stove
6. cup

7. bedroom
8. stairs
9. middle
10. waves
11. moon
12. pillow

MARGARET WISE BROWN: *The Runaway Bunny*

Answers may vary, but some possibilities are:

1. baseball glove
2. rain barrel
3. beehive
4. grapevine
5. squirrel

6. book shelf; library
7. zoo cage
8. ant hill
9. garage
10. stall; stable

PETER PARNALL: *The Mountain*

```
A C Z H B P Q U O A A E G U B E E I C
Z I D J O W S F Q A H W A U G O U L A
U K T L R J X L I T T E R L G O U K N
D D I J F W T V N D D H B O T T L E S
B I R D S J O Z B W W O A F F V H R G
J W O U T M D M R X P S G O Y M D K S
W K A B R J Y P S W A T E R F A L L D
D R D S E F H D E E R C Y E S C M E W
M W L K A L S J U N K Z V S H P X Z Y
E Y B I M O U N T A I N X T R A S H K
I C T P D W B P I C N I C Z I P G L A
R U S M P E O P L E G U I N T E W U G
F Q C X J R X P P H L N I H S R N D S
U M O L E S E C E B O H M W D A D B I
S D Q K X H S K K M T Z Y Y A R R E I
```

MARTHA ALEXANDER: *I'll Protect You from the Jungle Beasts*

1. beasts
2. lion
3. elephant
4. snake
5. hyena
6. bits

7. path
8. enormous
9. fever
10. weak
11. house
12. bed

MAY AUTHORS BIBLIOGRAPHY

May 4   Don Wood

With Audrey Wood as author, all are published by Harcourt Brace Jovanovich: *The Napping House* (1984); *Moonflute* (1986); *King Bidgood's in the Bathtub* (1986); *Heckedy Peg* (1987); *Elbert's Bad Word* (1988).

May 5   Leo Lionni

Inch by Inch (Astor-Honor, 1961)—1962 Caldecott Honor book; *Swimmy* (Pantheon, 1963)—1964 Caldecott Honor book; *Frederick* (Pantheon, 1967)—1968 Caldecott Honor book; *Alexander and the Wind-Up Mouse* (Pantheon, 1969)—1970 Caldecott Honor book; *Mouse Days: A Book of Seasons* (Pantheon, 1980); *Frederick's Fables: A Leo Lionni Treasury of Favorite Stories* (Pantheon, 1985); *Biggest House in the World* (Knopf, 1987); *Fish Is Fish* (Knopf, 1987).

May 6   Judy Delton

My Mom Hates Me in January (Whitman, 1977); *My Mother Lost Her Job Today* (Whitman, 1980); *I Never Win!* (Carolrhoda, 1981); *Groundhog's Day at the Doctor* (Parents, 1981); *The Goose Who Wrote a Book* (Carolrhoda, 1982); *Brimhall Turns Detective* (Carolrhoda, 1983); *A Birthday Bike for Brimhall* (Carolrholda, 1985); *The Elephant in Duck's Garden* (Whitman, 1985); *Two Good Friends* (Crown, 1986); *Rabbit Finds a Way* (Crown, 1986); *Rabbit Goes to Night School* (Whitman, 1986); *Rabbit's New Rug* (Crown, 1987).

May 6   Giulio Maestro

A Raft of Riddles (Dutton, 1982); *Riddles That Are a Scream* (Dutton, 1983); *Riddle Romp* (Houghton Mifflin, 1983); *Razzle-Dazzle Riddles* (Clarion, 1985); *What's a Frank Frank? Tasty Homograph Riddles* (Clarion, 1984); *What's Mite Might? Homophone* Riddles to Boost Your Word Power (CLarion, 1986).

May 7   Nonny Hogrogian

Illustrated *Always Room for One More* by Sorche Nic Leodhas (Holt, 1966)—1967 Caldecott Award winner, out of print; *One Fine Day* (Macmillan, 1971)—1972 Caldecott Award winner; *The Contest* (Greenwillow, 1976)—1977 Caldecott Honor book; *Noah's Ark* (Knopf, 1986).

May 9   James Barrie

Peter Pan (Macmillan, 1980); *Peter Pan* (Random, 1983).

May 9   Eleanor Estes

For third grade readers who need a challenge: *Witch Family* (HBJ, 1965); *Hundred Dresses* (HBJ, 1974); The Moffats series published by HBJ: *The Moffats, Middle Moffat, Moffat Museum.*

May 12   Edward Lear

The Complete Nonsense of Edward Lear (Amereon, Dodd, Mead, 1958—out of print); *An Edward Lear Alphabet* (Lothrop, 1983); *Nonsense Verse of Edward Lear* (Crown, 1984); *Scroobious Pip* (Harper, 1987).

May 14   George Selden

To read aloud or can be read by good third grade readers: *Harry Cat's Pet Puppy* (Farrar, 1974); *Harry Kitten and Tucker Mouse* (Farrar, 1986).

May 15   L. Frank Baum

The Wizard of Oz (Putnam, 1956); collection from Troll Associates for grades 1-2: *Dorothy and the Wicked Witch, Dorothy and the Wizard of Oz, Off to See the Wizard, Over the Rainbow*; *The Life and Adventures of Santa Claus* (New American Library, 1986).

May 15   Ellen MacGregor

Wrote Miss Pickerell series with Dora Pantell for third grade readers who want something different, published by McGraw-Hill: *Miss Pickerell & the Blue Whale, Miss Pickerell & the Super-Tanker, Miss Pickerell Meets Mr. H.U.M., Miss Pickerell on the Trail, Miss Pickerell Tackles the Energy Crisis, Miss Pickerell to the Earthquake Rescue*.

May 18   Lillian Hoban

All books published by Harper: *The Sugar Snow Spring* (1973); *Mr. Pig and Family* (1980); *The Case of the Two Masked Robbers* (1986); *Silly Tilly and the Easter Bunny* (1987); Arthur series: *Arthur's Pen Pal, Arthur's Prize Reader, Arthur's Loose Tooth, Arthur's Honey Bear, Arthur's Halloween Costume, Arthur's Funny Money, Arthur's Christmas Cookies*.

May 19   Thomas Feelings

Mojo Means One (Dial, 1971)—1972 Caldecott Honor book; *Jambo Means Hello* (Dial, 1974)—1975 Caldecott Honor book.

May 20   Carol Carrick

See "April 7, Donald Carrick" for listing.

May 22   Arnold Lobel

A classic storyteller and illustrator: *Giant John* (Harper, 1964); *Small Pig* (Harper, 1969); *Frog and Toad Are Friends* (Harper, 1970)—1971 Caldecott Honor book; *Hildilid's Night* (Macmillan, 1971)—1972 Caldecott Honor book; *Mouse Tales* (Harper, 1978); *Frog and Toad Together* (Harper, 1979); *Fables* (Harper, 1980)—1981 Caldecott Award winner; *Owl at Home* (Harper, 1982); *Ming Lo Moves the Mountain* (Greenwillow, 1982); *Mouse Soup* (Harper, 1983); *The Book of Pigericks* (Harper, 1983); *Days with Frog and Toad* (Harper, 1984); *Frog and Toad All Year* (Harper, 1984); *Whiskers and Rhymes* (Greenwillow,

1985); *Grasshopper on the Road* (Harper, 1986); *Lucille* (Harper, 1986); *Uncle Elephant* (Harper, 1986).

May 23   Margaret Wise Brown

Indoor Noisy Book (Harper, 1942); *Goodnight Moon* (Harper, 1947); *Quiet Noisy Book* (Harper, 1950); *The Runaway Bunny* (Harper, 1972); *Fox Eyes* (Pantheon, 1977—out of print); *Home for a Bunny* (Western, 1983); *The Little Fir Tree* (Harper, 1985).

May 23   Oliver Butterworth

The Enormous Egg (Dell, 1978).

May 23   Peter Parnall

The Mountain (Doubleday, 1971); *The Great Fish* (Doubleday, 1973); *Alfalfa Hill* (Doubleday, 1975); *Hawk, I Am Your Brother* (Macmillan, 1976)—1977 Caldecott Honor book; *Winter Barn* (Macmillan, 1986); also illustrated books for other authors: *Annie and the Old One* by Miska Miles (Little, Brown, 1971); *Everybody Needs a Rock* by Byrd Baylor (Macmillan, 1974); *If You Are a Hunter of Fossils* by Byrd Baylor (Macmillan, 1980); *The Way to Start a Day* by Byrd Baylor (Macmillan, 1986).

May 25   Martha Alexander

A prolific author/illustrator: *Blackboard Bear* (Dial, 1969); *We Never Get to Do Anything* (Dial, 1970); *And My Mean Old Mother Will Be Sorry, Blackboard Bear* (Dial, 1972); *I Sure Am Glad to See You, Blackboard Bear* (Dial, 1976); *Maybe a Monster* (Dial, 1979); *Marty McGee's Space Lab, No Girls Allowed* (Dial, 1981); *Move Over, Twerp* (Dial, 1981); *When the Baby Comes, I'm Moving Out* (Dial, 1981).

May 25   Bennett Cerf

Very funny collections of jokes and riddles: *Book of Laughs* (Random, 1959); *Book of Riddles* (Random, 1960); *More Riddles* (Random, 1961); *Book of Animal Riddles* (Random, 1964).

May 30   Millicent Selsam

Easy-to-read nonfiction for grades 1-3: *Terry and the Caterpillars* (Harper, 1962); *Greg's Microscope* (Harper, 1963); *Hidden Animals* (Harper, 1969); *Sea Monsters of Long Ago* (Macmillan, 1978); *All About Eggs* (Harper, 1980); *Cotton* (Morrow, 1982); *Catnip* (Morrow, 1983); *Is This a Baby Dinosaur?* (Harper, 1984); *Where Do They Go?—Insects in Winter* (Scholastic, 1984); *Egg to Chick* (Harper, 1987).

May 31   Jay Williams

Everyone Knows What a Dragon Looks Like (Macmillan, 1976); *The Reward Worth Having* (Macmillan, 1977); *The City Witch and the Country Witch*

(Macmillan, 1979); *One Big Wish* (Macmillan, 1980); Danny Dunn science fiction series written with Raymond Abrashkin for good third grade readers, published by Archway: *Danny Dunn & the Anti-Gravity Paint, DD & the Fossil Caves, DD & the Heat Ray, DD & the Homework Machine, DD & the Smallifying Machine, DD & the Swamp Monster, DD & the Universal Glue, DD & the Voice from Space, DD & the Weather Machine.*

May 31   Elizabeth Coatsworth

For third grade readers who like a challenge: *The Cat Who Went to Heaven* (Macmillan, 1967)—1931 Newbery Award winner; *Marra's World* (Greenwillow, 1975).

JUNE

June 1   James Daugherty, *Andy and the Lion* (fill-in)

June 2   Paul Galdone, *The Amazing Pig* (writing activity)

June 3   Anita Lobel, *Potatoes, Potatoes* (word meanings)

June 6   Peter Spier, *Noah's Ark* (listing Noah's chores)

June 6   Verna Aardema, *Who's in Rabbit's House?* (rewriting)

June 14   Janice May Udry, *A Tree Is Nice* (writing activity)

June 17   Beatrice Schenk DeRegniers, *May I Bring a Friend?* (writing rhymes)

June 18   Chris Van Allsbury, *The Polar Express* (suggested use)

          Chris Van Allsburg, *Mysteries of Harris Burdick* (story-starter)

June 21   Robert Kraus, *How Spider Saved Halloween* (drawing activity)

June 25   Eric Carle, *The Very Hungry Caterpillar* (magic foods)

June 26   Nancy Willard, *Papa's Panda* (writing activity)

June 26   Charlotte Zolotow, *Someday* (writing activity)

June 30   David McPhail, *Emma's Vacation* (fill-in)

    June Bookmarks
    June Answer Key
    June Authors Bibliography

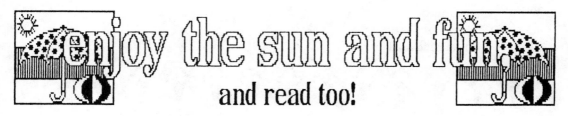

enjoy the sun and fun
and read too!

JUNE AUTHORS

DATE	NAME	AUTHOR/ILLUSTRATOR		READING LEVEL			
				K	1	2	3
1	James Daugherty	X	X		X	X	X
2	Paul Galdone		X			X	X
3	Anita Lobel	X	X			X	X
5	Richard Scarry	X	X	X	X		
6	Verna Aardema	X		X	X	X	
6	Cynthia Rylant	X			X	X	X
6	Peter Spier	X	X	X	X	X	X
7	Georgess McHargue	X					X
10	Maurice Sendak	X	X	X	X	X	X
14	Janice May Udry	X		X	X	X	
17	Beatrice Schenk De Regniers	X		X	X	X	
18	Pat Hutchins	X	X	X	X		
18	Chris Van Allsburg	X	X	X	X	X	X
21	Robert Kraus	X		X	X	X	
24	Linda Glovach	X			X	X	X
25	Eric Carle	X	X	X	X	X	
25	Elizabeth Orton Jones		X	X	X		
26	Robert Burch	X			X	X	
26	Lynd Ward	X	X	X	X	X	X
26	Nancy Willard	X	X	X	X	X	X
26	Charlotte Zolotow	X		X	X	X	X
29	Antoine de Saint Exupery	X			X	X	X
30	David McPhail	X	X	X	X	X	

JAMES DAUGHERTY

"Andy and the Lion"

Read "Andy and the Lion." Use the words in the Word Bank to finish these sentences about a little boy who is kind to a lion.

1. Andy went to the _____.

2. He checked out a book about _____.

3. His grandfather hunted lions in _____.

4. Andy _____ about lions that night.

5. Andy met a lion on the way to _____.

6. The lion had a _____ in his _____.

7. Andy removed it with a pair of _____.

8. In the spring, the _____ came to town.

9. A lion _____ out of the _____.

10. It was Andy's _____.

11. Andy got a medal for _____.

12. Andy returned the _____ to the library.

WORD BANK

Africa	book	bravery	cage	circus	dreamed	friend
jumped	library	lions	paw	pliers	school	thorn

Name_____ Date_____

PAUL GALDONE

"The Amazing Pig"

Read "The Amazing Pig." Paul retold the story of a very amazing pig. The young boy was very proud of the family pig. What kind of animal would you be proud to have as a pet. What amazing things would it do? Write a story about your amazing imaginary pet. Answer these questions to help you get started.

What kind of amazing pet will you have?

_____

What does it do that is so unusual?

_____

_____

_____

How does it know how to do this?

_____

_____

_____

I want to buy your pet for a million dollars. Would you sell it? Why or why not?

_____

_____

Name_____ **Date**_____

ANITA LOBEL

"Potatoes, Potatoes"

Read "Potatoes, Potatoes." Match the words in the Word Bank to their word meanings below.

1. ___ ___ ___   when countries fight
2. ___ ___ ___ ___ ___   weapon
3. ___ ___ ___ ___ ___ ___   grows underground
4. ___ ___ ___ ___   stone fence
5. ___ ___ ___ ___   group of soldiers
6. ___ ___ ___ ___ ___ ___ ___   leader of army
7. ___ ___ ___ ___ ___   award for bravery
8. ___ ___ ___ ___ ___ ___   when armies fight
9. ___ ___ ___ ___ ___ ___   wanting food
10. ___ ___ ___ ___ ___ ___ ___   win a battle
11. ___ ___ ___ ___ ___   no fighting
12. ___ ___ ___ ___   put underground

WORD BANK

army	battle	bury	general	hungry	medal
peace	potato	sword	victory	wall	war

Name_____ **Date**_____

PETER SPIER

"Noah's Ark"

_____

    Read and look at the pictures in "Noah's Ark." There are some everyday things that Noah had to do to take care of all those animals. Peter Spier didn't write about them. He drew pictures of them. Make a list of all the chores Noah had to do. Be very specific.

_____

_____

_____

_____

_____

_____

_____

_____

_____

_____

_____

_____

_____

_____

Name_____   **Date**_____

VERNA AARDEMA

"Who's in Rabbit's House?"

Read "Who's in Rabbit's House." Now that you have read this African play, ask your teacher if you and several others can perform it too. You need to do several things first.

1. Rewrite this story so that it looks like a play. You will need a narrator for the beginning, the parts that no characters speak, and the parts between the actors' speeches.

   NARRATOR:
   RABBIT:
   FROG:
   JACKAL:
   LEOPARD:
   ELEPHANT:
   RHINOCEROUS:
   LONG ONE:

2. There will be eight actors in this play. Decide who will read each part. You need not memorize the parts. You can just read them. You can make masks if you want and add a few simple props: cardboard hut, blue material for the lake, sticks etc.

3. Have fun presenting it to your class.

4. Make several presentations for other classrooms and grade levels. They'll enjoy this original African look at humor.

Name _____   Date _____

JANICE UDRY

"A Tree Is Nice"

_____

Read "A Tree Is Nice." Trees are nice. Hills are nice. Snow is nice too. There are many nice things. Write a story to share with your friends about the thing you think is nice. Answer these questions to help you start.

Trees are helpful. How is your nice thing helpful?

_____

_____

_____

_____

Trees are beautiful. How is your nice thing beautiful?

_____

_____

_____

_____

Trees are fun to play in, on, near, or with. How is your nice thing fun to play with?

_____

_____

Now write your story so we can learn about and enjoy your nice thing.

Name_____   **Date**_____

BEATRICE SCHENK DEREGNIERS

"May I Bring a Friend?"

Read "May I Bring a Friend?" This famous Caldecott Award winner has beautiful pictures and the following animals: giraffe, hippopotamus, monkeys, elephant, lions, and a seal. Beatrice could have picked other animals.

Pick five of the following creatures and make a short rhyme to tell us what they ate at the tea party with the King and Queen. Read the examples for help.

EXAMPLES

Miss Goose slurped a strawberry mousse and spilled her milk on poor Mister Moose.

Mr. Eel made a big deal out of the brown spots on his banana peel. The hyena laughed, and said, "Are you daft? The brown part makes you smart!"

1. ant, bee, cat, dog, eel, fox, goose, hyena, iguana, jackal, leopard, moose, octopus, rat, snake, turtle, vole whale, yak, zebra

Pick your creatures and GET BUSY!

_____

_____

_____

_____

_____

Name_____ **Date**_____

CHRIS VAN ALLSBURG

"The Polar Express"

FOR THE TEACHER, LIBRARIAN, MEDIA SPECIALIST

In order to make Van Allsburg's "Polar Express" a truly memorable experience, follow these directions:

Wear a bell around your neck and ring it at appropriate times in the story.

After you finish the story, give the boys and girls a little silver bell on a strand of curling ribbon.

I have read and given bells for a number of years now. And in every class, there are several children who wear their bell the week before Christmas. They always ask, "Do you remember?" And I always say, "Yes, but it's most important that you do." And they do!

CHRIS VAN ALLSBURG

"The Mysteries of Harris Burdick"

Look at all the pictures Chris Van Allsburg has created for you in "The Mysteries of Harris Burdick." The introduction states that a certain Harris Burdick stopped at a publisher's office one day. He had 14 pictures with him that went with stories he had at home. He promised to return the next day with the stories. He left the pictures with the publisher. The publisher never saw Harris Burdick again.

If there really were stories to go with these captioned pictures, what were they? I guess we'll just have to make up some stories of our own.

Look for the picture called "Uninvited Guests." Why is the man going downstairs? What time is it? What time of year is it? What in this world or another is behind that little door? Why is he in that house?

I will start this story for you. You finish it *or* pick another picture and write a story to go with it.

Uninvited Guests

It was late. Almost midnight, if I remember. The storm was raging, wind was howling like the devil's own voice. There was a snap and a crack. The lights went out.

As I opened the door to the basement, it creaked, but not loud enough to muffle the slamming of a door. At least I thought it was a door.

I let it go as my imagination. It was only my third night in the house. If I could stay two more days, I'd collect a fortune. My grandfather's will said I had to stay for five days and nights alone.

I was three stairs from the bottom, when I saw the door. I didn't see it when I moved in. But there it was. And then the knob turned. Light came from the other side as IT looked at me.

I didn't run. I didn't scream. I said "...

Name _____   Date _____

CHRIS VAN ALLSBURG

Directions for Doorway of "Uninvited Guests"

Your story about "Uninvited Guests" from *The Mysteries of Harris Burdick* can be written on the worksheet with the same name. You can also glue that sheet to the "door" sheet to give your story an illustration of what the guests look like. Follow these simple steps.

1. Cut the door opening from the bottom left to the top right. Stop at the hinges.
2. Place the "Uninvited Guests" lined paper face down on a table with the heading closest to you.
3. Place the "door" worksheet on top of the other sheet with the door facing up and closest to you.
4. Glue the sheets together.
5. Fold the sheet in half so the door is on the top.
6. Open the door. You have a space to draw the "Uninvited Guests"
7. Open the sheet and you have room to write your little story.

Have fun with the drawing, writing, and being creative!

© 1989 by The Center for Applied Research in Education

Name _____   **Date** _____

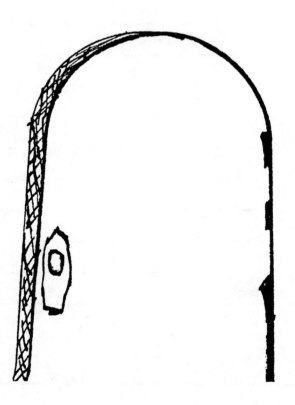

Uninvited Guests

_____

_____

_____

_____

_____

_____

_____

_____

_____

_____

_____

_____

_____

_____

_____

_____

_____

_____

_____

_____

_____

Name_____ **Date**_____

ROBERT KRAUS

"How Spider Saved Halloween"

Read "How Spider Saved Halloween." Robert Kraus can draw too! Robert created a very simple character called spider. You can create a character too. And draw him or her.

Think about a character that you can draw easily. My little character is a troll. Draw your character in the frame to the right. Answer the questions below and on the next page. They will help you set up a story. Write the story. Have fun!

What's your character's name?

_____

What does it like to do?

_____

Name_____ **Date**_____

ROBERT KRAUS

Does it have any friends? What are they and what are their names?

_____   _____

_____   _____

What problem comes up? _____

_____

How will it be solved?

_____

_____

Draw the pictures for your own story. If Robert Kraus can do it—so can you!

Name_____   **Date**_____

ERIC CARLE

"The Very Hungry Caterpillar"

Read "The Very Hungry Caterpillar." All this talk about food has made me very hungry. There is a saying, "You are what you eat." Perhaps all the butterfly's beautiful colors came from the pretty colors in the foods he ate.

Let's pretend food does very strange things to us—perhaps, magically strange things. Use the words in the Word Bank to answer these questions about "magic food."

1. What would you eat to be very sweet? _____

2. What would a sour puss eat? _____

3. What would a grouchy person eat? _____

4. What would make you light enough to float? _____

   _____

5. What would make you bark? _____

6. What would make you cackle like a hen? _____

7. What would make you a good swimmer? _____

8. What would make you hop? _____.

9. What would make elephants follow you? _____

10. What would make you moo? _____

WORD BANK

candy	cotton candy	crab	eggs	fish
hot dogs	lemons	milk	peanut butter	rabbit stew

Write about other "magic foods" on the back of this page. Example: If carrots make you orange, what makes you green?

Name _____ **Date** _____

NANCY WILLARD

"Papa's Panda"

_____

    Read "Papa's Panda." Papa and Jim have a wonderful time imagining that a panda is coming to visit them. Notice how Nancy Willard lets us know what pandas eat as part of the story. We also know they come from China. Even though this is a fiction book, we know something about pandas when we finish reading it. Write your own story about the animal you would like most to visit you. Use these questions to help you think before you write.

1. What animal is coming to visit you? _____.

2. How will the animal get to your house?

_____

3. What will it eat at your house?

_____

4. Where will your visitor sleep? _____

5. What kinds of games will your animal play?

_____

6. What other special things will it need?

_____

_____

_____

Name_____   **Date**_____

CHARLOTTE ZOLOTOW

"Someday"

_____

Read "Someday." If we are lucky, we will all be older someday. Finish these sentences about your someday to come.

1. Someday, I will be a _____.

2. Then I will be able to

_____

_____

or

_____

3. Someday, I'll give my mom a _____

4. Someday, I'll give my dad a _____

5. Someday, I'll give my brother or sister a _____

6. Someday, I'll _____.

7. Someday, I'll _____.

8. Someday, I'll _____.

9. Someday, I'll _____.

10. Someday, I'll _____.

11. Someday, I'll _____.

12. Someday, I'll _____.

Name _____ **Date** _____

DAVID MCPHAIL

"Emma's Vacation"

Read "Emma's Vacation." Use the words in the Word Bank to finish these sentences about a little bear who goes on a vacation.

1. Emma went on a _____ with her parents.

2. The ride was _____ and they got _____.

3. It _____ and the _____ leaked.

4. Emma wanted to _____ the mountain.

5. They _____ the car instead.

6. They went out to _____ at a hamburger place.

7. They rode on a _____ and in a _____.

8. They took a ride on a _____.

9. The next day, they waded in a _____.

10. They caught _____ and picked _____.

11. That night, they sang _____ in a _____.

12. Emma had a _____ day.

WORD BANK					
berries	boat	brook	bus	climb	drove
fish	hammock	long	lost	lunch	rained
roof	songs	train	vacation	wonderful	

Name_____   Date_____

JUNE READERS

WE LOVE OUR DADS!

CHILL OUT WITH A

GOOD BOOK

IT'S FUN

TO READ IN THE SUN

BOOKS GO TO CAMP TOO

BOOKS HELP YOU SOAR!

JUNE ANSWER KEY

JAMES DAUGHERTY: *Andy and the Lion*

1. library
2. lions
3. Africa
4. dreamed
5. school
6. thorn; paw
7. pliers
8. circus
9. jumped; cage
10. friend
11. bravery
12. book

ANITA LOBEL: *Potatoes, Potatoes*

1. war
2. sword
3. potato
4. wall
5. army
6. general
7. medal
8. battle
9. hungry
10. victory
11. peace
12. bury

ERIC CARLE: *The Very Hungry Caterpillar*

1. candy
2. lemons
3. crab
4. cotton candy
5. hot dogs
6. eggs
7. fish
8. rabbit stew
9. peanut butter
10. milk

DAVID McPHAIL: *Emma's Vacation*

1. vacation
2. long; lost
3. rained; roof
4. climb
5. drove
6. lunch
7. train; boat
8. bus
9. brook
10. fish; berries
11. songs; hammock
12. wonderful

JUNE AUTHORS BIBLIOGRAPHY

June 1   James Daugherty

Andy and the Lion (Viking, 1938)—1939 Caldecott Honor book; *Daniel Boone* (Viking, 1939—out of print)—1940 Newbery Award winner.

June 2   Paul Galdone

Illustrated many fairy tales published by Clarion: *The Elves and the Shoemaker, The Gingerbread Boy, Jack and the Beanstalk, The Amazing Pig, The Turtle and the Monkey.*

June 3   Anita Lobel

Sven's Bridge (Harper, 1965); *King Rooster, Queen Hen* (Greenwillow, 1975); *The Straw Maid* (Greenwillow, 1983); *Potatoes, Potatoes* (Harper, 1984); illustrated *The Rose in My Garden* by Arnold Lobel (Greenwillow, 1984).

June 5   Richard Scarry

Over 45 books to choose from, including: *Best Mother Goose Ever* (Western Publishing, 1970); *ABC Word Book* (Random, 1971); *Early Words* (Random, 1976); *Best Christmas Book Ever* (Random, 1981).

June 6   Verna Aardema

Why Mosquitoes Buzz in People's Ears, Illustrated by Leo and Diane Dillon (Dial, 1975)—1976 Caldecott Award winner; *Who's in Rabbit's House?* illustrated by Leo and Diane Dillon (Dial, 1977).

June 6   Cynthia Rylant

When I Was Young in the Mountains (Dutton, 1982)—1983 Caldecott Award winner; *This Year's Garden* (Bradbury, 1984); *The Relatives Came* (Bradbury, 1985); *Night in the Country* (Bradbury, 1986); *Birthday Presents* (Orchard, 1987); Henry and Mudge series published by Bradbury.

June 6   Peter Spier

Fox Went Out on a Chilly Night (Doubleday, 1961)—1962 Caldecott Honor book; *Tin Lizzie* (Doubleday, 1975); *Noah's Ark* (Doubleday, 1977)—1978 Caldecott Award winner: *Oh, Were They Ever Happy* (Doubleday, 1978); *People* (Doubleday, 1980); *Rain* (Doubleday, 1982); *Christmas* (Doubleday, 1983); *Dreams* (Doubleday, 1986); *We the People* (Doubleday, 1987).

June 7   Georgess McHargue

Meet the Werewolf (Lippincott, 1976); *Meet the Vampire* (Lippincott, 1979); *Meet the Witches* (Lippincott, 1984); these are out of print, but they may still be on the library shelves: *The Impossible People, Beasts of Never, Funny Bananas*; *Mystery in the Museum*.

June 10   Maurice Sendak

What Do You Say, Dear (Scholastic, 1980)—1959 Caldecott Honor book; *Alligators All Around* (Harper, 1962); *Chicken Soup with Rice* (Harper, 1962); *One Was Johnny* (Harper, 1962); *Outside Over There* (Harper, 1962); *Pierre* (Harper, 1962); *Where the Wild Things Are* (Harper, 1962)—1964 Caldecott Award winner; *In the Night Kitchen* (Harper, 1970).

June 14   Janice May Udry

A Tree Is Nice (Harper, 1956)—1957 Caldecott Award winner; *Moon Jumpers*, illustrated by Maurice Sendak (Harper, 1959)—1960 Caldecott Honor book; *Let's Be Enemies* (Harper, 1961).

June 17   Beatrice Schenk DeRegniers

May I Bring a Friend? (Macmillan, 1964)—1965 Caldecott Award winner; *Laura's Story* (Atheneum, 1979); *Waiting for Mama* (Houghton Mifflin, 1984); *So Many Cats* (Clarion, 1985).

June 18   Pat Hutchins

Rosie's Walk (Macmillan, 1971); *Titch* (Macmillan, 1971); *Good-Night Owl* (Macmillan, 1972); *The Wind Blew* (Macmillan, 1974); *Don't Forget the Bacon!* (Greenwillow, 1976); *The Best Train Set Ever* (Greenwillow, 1978); *Happy Birthday, Sam* (Greenwillow, 1978); *The Tale of Thomas Mead* (Greenwillow, 1980); *One Hunter* (Greenwillow, 1982); *You'll Soon Grow into Them, Titch* (Greenwillow, 1983); *The Curse of the Egyptian Mummy* (Greenwillow, 1983); *King Henry's Palace* (Greenwillow, 1983); *The Very Worst Monster* (Greenwillow, 1985); *Surprise Party* (Macmillan, 1986); *The Doorbell Rang* (Greenwillow, 1986); *Changes, Changes* (Macmillan, 1987).

June 18   Chris Van Allsburg

Garden of Abdul Gasazi (Houghton Mifflin, 1979)—1980 Caldecott Honor book; *Jumanji* (Houghton Mifflin, 1981)—1982 Caldecott Award winner; *Ben's Dream* (Houghton Mifflin, 1982); *The Wreck of the Zephyr* (Houghton Mifflin, 1983); *Mysteries of Harris Burdick* (Houghton Mifflin, 1984); *The Polar Express* (Houghton Mifflin, 1985)—1986 Caldecott Award winner; *The Stranger* (Houghton Mifflin, 1986); *The Z Was Zapped: A Play in Twenty-Six Acts* (Houghton Mifflin, 1987).

June 21   Robert Kraus

Leo the Late Bloomer (Crowell, 1971); *Whose Mouse Are You?* (Macmillan, 1972); *Herman the Helper* (Troll, 1974); *Milton the Early Riser* (Messner, 1981); *Where Are You Going, Little Mouse* (Greenwillow, 1986); *How Spider Saved Halloween* (Scholastic, 1986); *How Spider Saved Turkey* (Troll, 1986); *How*

Spider Saved Valentine's Day (Scholastic, 1986); *Mrs. Elmo of Elephant House* (Delacorte, 1986); *Spider's First Day at School* (Scholastic, 1987); *The Hoodwinking of Mrs. Elmo* (Delacorte, 1989).

June 24   Linda Glovach

Little Witch fun-to-make-and-do books published by Prentice Hall: *Little Witch's Birthday Book, Little Witch's Black Magic Book of Disguises, Little Witch's Black Magic Book of Games, Little Witch's Black Magic Cookbook, Little Witch's Cat Book.*

June 25   Eric Carle

Grouchy Ladybug (Crowell, 1977); *The Very Hungry Caterpillar* (Putnam, 1981); *Mixed-Up Chameleon* (Crowell, 1984); *The Very Busy Spider* (Putnam, 1984); My Very First series published by Harper: *My Very First Book of Colors, ...Food, ...Growth, ...Heads and Tails, ...Homes, ...Motion, ...Numbers, ...Shapes, ...Sounds, ...Tools, ...Touch, ...Words.*

June 25   Elizabeth Orton Jones

Illustrated *Prayer for a Child* by Rachel Field (Macmillan, 1968)—1945 Caldecott Award winner.

June 26   Robert Burch

Skinny (Dell, 1970); *Ida Early Comes over the Mountain* (Viking, 1980); *Christmas with Ida Early* (Viking, 1983); *King Kong and Other Poets* (Viking, 1986).

June 26   Lynd Ward

The Biggest Bear (Houghton Mifflin, 1952)—1953 Caldecott Award winner; *Silver Pony: A Story in Pictures* (Houghton Mifflin, 1973).

June 26   Nancy Willard

Stranger's Bread (HBJ, 1977); *Simple Pictures Are Best* (HBJ, 1978); *Papa's Panda* (HBJ, 1979); *Marzipan Moon* (HBJ, 1981); *A Visit to William Blake's Inn: Poems for Innocent and Experienced Travelers* (HBJ, 1981)—1982 Newbery Medal winner and Caldecott Honor book; *Night Story* (HBJ, 1986); *Mountain of Quilt* (HBJ, 1987).

June 26   Charlotte Zolotow

Over 40 titles, including: *Bunny Who Found Easter* (Houghton Mifflin, 1959); *Mr. Rabbit and the Lovely Present*, illustrated by Maurice Sendak (Harper, 1962)—1963 Caldecott Honor book; *Someday* (Harper, 1965); *If It Weren't for You* (Harper, 1966); *Quarreling Book* (Harper, 1982); *Beautiful Christmas Tree* (Houghton Mifflin, 1983).

June 29   Antoine de Saint Exupery

The Little Prince (HBJ, 1943).

June Authors Bibliography

June 30   David McPhail

    Snow Lion (Parents, 1983); *Fix-It* (Dutton, 1984); *Sisters* (HBJ, 1984); *Emma's Pet* (Dutton, 1985); *Farm Morning* (HBJ, 1985); *Dream Child* (Dutton, 1985); *Emma's Vacation* (Dutton, 1987); Pig Pig series published by Dutton: *Pig Pig Rides, Pig Pig Goes to Camp, Pig Pig Grows Up, Pig Pig & the Magic Photo Album.*

JULY

WE LOVE READING
IN THE U.S.A.

JULY AUTHORS

DATE	NAME	AUTHOR	ILLUSTRATOR	K	1	2	3
2	Jack Gantos	X			X	X	
10	Julian May is also Ian Thorne	X				X	X
10	Martin Provensen	X	X	X	X	X	X
11	E.B. White	X					X
13	Marcia Brown	X		X	X		
14	Peggy Parish	X		X	X	X	
15	Clement Moore	X		X	X	X	
15	Walter Edmonds	X				X	X
16	Richard Egielski		X	X	X	X	
16	Eve Titus	X				X	X
19	Eve Merriam	X		X	X	X	X
22	Margery Williams	X		X	X	X	X
23	Patricia Coombs	X		X	X	X	
23	Robert Quackenbush	X	X			X	X
26	Jan Berenstain	X		X	X	X	
27	Scott Corbett	X					X
28	Natalie Babbitt	X		X	X	X	X
28	Beatrix Potter	X	X	X	X	X	X
31	Muriel Feelings		X	X	X	X	

JACK GANTOS

"Rotten Ralph"

Read "Rotten Ralph." Use the words in the Word Bank to finish these sentences about a very nasty, nasty cat.

1. Ralph was a _____ cat.
2. He made _____ of Sarah when she practiced _____.
3. He took a _____ out of each party _____.
4. He sat in her father's favorite _____.
5. He chased mother's favorite _____.
6. They went to the _____ one night.
7. He knocked over the tightrope _____.
8. Sarah's father made Ralph _____ there.
9. The monkeys threw banana _____ at him.
10. The elephants shot _____ at him.
11. Ralph _____ from the circus.
12. Sarah finally found him in an _____ and took him _____. She loved him anyway.

```
WORD BANK
alley      ballet     birds      bite      chair
circus     cookie     escaped    fun       home
peanuts    peels      rotten     stay      walkers
```

Name _____   Date _____

MARTIN PROVENSEN

"The Year at Maple Hill Farm"

Read and look at all the pictures in "The Year at Maple Hill Farm." There are so many things that go on at a farm through the year. The farmers and their families always have something to do. Even the animals are busy.

1. Pick your favorite month or season. Make a list of everything the farmers and the animals do.

2. Why is that season your favorite? Make a list of reasons.

3. If you went to live on the farm for your favorite season, what would you need to take with you. Make a list.

4. What would you leave at home? Make a list.

5. Write a short, little story about being on a farm during your favorite season.

Name_____ **Date**_____

MARCIA BROWN

"Once a Mouse"

_____

Read "Once a Mouse." Use the words in the Word Bank to finish these sentences about a little mouse who forgets where he started. There is an expression "pride before the fall." After you read this story, you will understand what it means.

1. A magical hermit sat one day thinking about _____ and _____.
2. A _____ tried to catch a mouse.
3. Then a _____ tried to eat the hermit's pet.
4. He _____ the mouse into a cat.
5. He changed that cat into a _____.
6. Then it became a _____.
7. The tiger was very _____.
8. He didn't want to be _____ that he was a mouse.
9. The tiger planned to _____ the hermit.
10. The hermit changed him back into a _____.
11. People should be _____.
12. They should be _____ for what others do for them.

WORD BANK						
big	crow	cat	changed	dog	grateful	humble
kill	little	mouse	proud	reminded	tiger	

Name_____ Date_____

PEGGY PARISH

"Play Ball, Amelia Bedelia"

Read "Play Ball, Amelia Bedelia." Amelia sometimes confuses what words mean. That's normal. Some words have more than one meaning. Write two definitions for each word; a dictionary definition and a baseball definition.

1. warm up _____

2. steal _____

3. tag _____

4. put out _____

5. plate _____

6. run home _____

7. keep score _____

Name_____ **Date**_____

WALTER EDMONDS

"The Matchlock Gun"

Read "The Spanish Gun" from "The Matchlock Gun." Find the words from Chapter One in the Word Search puzzle below

```
Y U O N Z L Z V S G F U Z G F F V T M J F
X I H A P F U R S A R T M L F I W B W T T
O J E W P X M U S K E T R F N B R N W N Q
Y R R V Y Q L T Q N N J E G W L O E I S S
U X R C I W O F G A C Y K U I N N L U D W
A R D F I O L I U U H J V U N I F O R M S
G F S I B T I J N Y H L Y A T I Q V A A H
R W Z K T S W Y G D T O C A E M S C C W N
V J U Z V S Y Q Z E I M L L R Z D J U Y N
S L A F A V U Q T D R A I L J L T R D I L
W W A G C E P I E H P T N L A H J U P H H
B M Z T I U B J Z G O C R S I N R S O G J
K T I Y X W B H N L W H O U A T D W G L I
Y L Y O O T A F C T D L O C D K I L R W H
H K I Z R D A A H R E O V J Q E P A G K V
Y N S D J N T Q A L R C G J B V D J E Q N
N P J N L L P W B X Q K Y B Y Z J L Q P D
X Z M J W K D Y S M O L O O H G Z H X R W
B R I D G E M A H T F Z S S M J X O L V N
```

WORD BANK						
boots	bridge	cannon	Edward	fire	flint	French
Gertrude	gun	Holland	Indians	matchlock	militia	musket
Palatine	powder	Teunis	Trudy	uniform	winter	

Name _____   Date _____

CLEMENT C. MOORE

"The Night Before Christmas"

FOR THE TEACHER, LIBRARIAN, MEDIA SPECIALIST

Make a special note for displaying "The Night Before Christmas" by Clement C. Moore illustrated by Tasha Tudor.

This special edition Rand McNally, 1975 is a collection of alternating watercolors and pencil sketches. In addition to illustrating the specific story theme, Tasha adds her own delicate story line with outside animals: owl, chipmunk, etc. helping Santa. Inside the house, a cat and a dog help Santa. With the magic of Christmas Eve, a clown and doll come to life.

"The Night Before Christmas" is a must, but this edition is truly special.

There are equally superb editions by other well-known illustrators listed in the July Author Bibliography.

Display them all and vote for the classroom favorite.

RICHARD EGIELSKI

"Mary's Mirror"

Read "Mary's Mirror." Use the words in the Word Bank to finish these sentences about a little girl who discovers she can be happy just the way she is. Notice the mirror Richard drew. What scary creature do you see in the frame of the mirror?

1. Mary was poor, but she was _____.

2. One day she found a _____.

3. Then she didn't like the way she _____.

4. She traded her clock for a _____.

5. She traded her cat for a _____.

6. She traded her doves for leather _____.

7. She got two _____ for her flute.

8. She got a golden _____ for all her grain.

9. Her happiness didn't _____.

10. She went to town and _____ everything back.

11. She went home and _____ that mirror.

12. She played a _____ on her flute and danced.

13. She was _____, but happy once more

WORD BANK

boots	broke	chain	frock	gloves	happy
hat	last	looked	mirror	song	traded
poor					

Name _____ Date _____

EVE MERRIAM

"Good Night to Annie"

Read "Good Night to Annie." It is a wonderful, soft, sleepy story. Let's write a good night book for the kindergarten children in your school. Let's pick animals that Eve didn't pick.

1. Pick an animal that starts with each letter of the alphabet.

2. Write a phrase or sentence that tells how the animal sleeps or gets ready to sleep.

3. Put each sentence on its own page and draw a picture to go with it.

Here are some examples for you.

Anacondas wriggle round and round and finally settle down.

Bears snuggle cozy in their earthen cave.

Chickens and chicks flip-flop and hop to their roost clucking softly "Move over, mom."

Please finish.

Name_____   Date_____

MARGERY WILLIAMS

"The Velveteen Rabbit: Or How Toys Become Real"

Read "The Velveteen Rabbit: Or How Toys Become Real." Find the words from the Word Bank in the word search puzzle below.

```
L W B Z L G C C L L X B G X S P B K W
V T D A U I T O C G J M C K J I F X R
J U E D G H W B U S O Z X J G B S S I
G R W A A T K H Z S R N Y S Q Y U Y P
B X M N R A B B I T M W H C B T N L X
V G W C D R H W E S Z R B F D F O C A
Q I V E E S P U M Z P V T F O D C X X
R A P K N P A K I S S E D L A V O J F
Y T F T G L G B Q N L L R U U I N Y O
Z H P O G C T U O R Y V E S F B R G A
F Q T J P V Y N A S T E O R N E Z Y H
U F W F A T L C J F Z T Y U S M V K U
B U R R O W S H G W W E U R U C C E E
X K R R Q I A Y A M E E U V U I K K R
B D Q O K T Y R P I C N I C S V R G T
Q S B P U C A O W V M M G I Q G X V M
P P W G P H H L Z D O K T I D E F L D
X M P I H R Z J K S L I E L D A C C P
```

WORD BANK

bunchy	burrows	dance	dew	fairy	fat	fever
garden	hop	hug	kissed	magic	nursery	picnics
rabbit	real	scarlet	talk	tear	twitch	whispers
velveteen						

Name _____   Date _____

PATRICIA COOMBS

"Dorrie and the Blue Witch"

Read "Dorrie and the Blue Witch." Match the words in the Word Bank to their meanings below.

1. ___ ___ ___ ___ ___ ___ ___   not straight

2. ___ ___ ___ ___ ___ ___ ___   place to cook at home

3. ___ ___ ___ ___ ___ ___   make smaller

4. ___ ___ ___ ___ ___   like a cape

5. ___ ___ ___ ___   closed hand

6. ___ ___ ___   buzzing insect

7. ___ ___ ___ ___ ___ ___   glass container

8. ___ ___ ___ ___ ___   instrument with keys

9. ___ ___ ___ ___ ___ ___   has good manners

10. ___ ___ ___ ___ ___ ___ ___ ___   big, black kettle

WORD BANK				
bee	bottle	cauldron	cloak	crooked
fist	kitchen	piano	polite	shrink

Name _____   **Date** _____

ROBERT QUACKENBUSH

"Dig to Disaster"

Read "Dig to Disaster." Answer the Who, What, Where, How, When, and Why questions about this mystery.

1. Who believed in the headless demon? _____

2. What happened to the bridge? _____

3. What happened to the canoe? _____

4. Who read the correct date on the Mayan temple? _____

5. What sound did everyone hear? _____

6. What did they see? _____

7. What clue did Miss Mallard find in the dirt? _____

8. How did she "open the mountain"? _____

9. Who was the demon? _____

10. Why did he want to scare everyone away? _____

_____

Name_____ Date_____

JAN BERENSTAIN

"The Berenstain Bears Go to Camp"

Read "The Berenstain Bears Go to Camp." Match the words in the Word Bank to their definitions below.

1. ___ ___ ___ ___ ___ ___ ___ ___   rest time

2. ___ ___ ___ ___   fun away from home

3. ___ ___ ___ ___   giant pool of water

4. ___ ___ ___ ___   cut tree trunks

5. ___ ___ ___ ___   laws

6. ___ ___ ___ ___ ___   boat to paddle

7. ___ ___ ___ ___ ___   holds a picture

8. ___ ___ ___ ___   hole in the ground

9. ___ ___ ___ ___ ___ ___   old story

10. ___ ___ ___ ___ ___ ___   award

WORD BANK				
camp	canoe	cave	frame	lake
legend	logs	rules	trophy	vacation

Name_____   Date_____

BEATRIX POTTER

"The Tale of Peter Rabbit"

Read "The Tale of Peter Rabbit." Use the words in the Word Bank to finish these sentences about a little rabbit who doesn't listen to his mother very well.

1. Peter lived under a fir _____.

2. Mother said, "Don't go to the _____."

3. Peter's father ended up in a _____.

4. Mrs. Rabbit went to the _____.

5. _____ went to McGregor's garden.

6. He ate _____, _____, and _____.

7. Mr. McGregor chased after Peter with a _____.

8. Peter lost one of his _____.

9. Peter hid in a watering _____.

10. Finally, Peter found the _____.

11. Peter caught a _____.

12. Mother gave him some _____ and put him to _____.

WORD BANK

bakery	beans	bed	cold	garden	gate	lettuce
Peter	pie	radishes	rake	shoes	tea	tree
can						

Name_____ **Date**_____

JULY READERS

OOH AAH OOH AAH READ!

FREEDOM
TO READ!

READ
AND BE PROUD

WE WANT YOU
TO READ!

WE, THE PEOPLE
LOVE TO READ!

JULY ANSWER KEY

JACK GANTOS: *Rotten Ralph*

1. rotten
2. fun; ballet
3. bite; cookie
4. chair
5. birds
6. circus

7. walkers
8. stay
9. peels
10. peanuts
11. escaped
12. alley; home

MARCIA BROWN: *Once a Mouse*

1. big; little
2. crow
3. cat
4. changed
5. dog
6. tiger

7. proud
8. reminded
9. kill
10. mouse
11. humble
12. grateful

PEGGY PARISH: *Play Ball, Amelia Bedelia*

1. (a) to heat up; (b) to loosen muscles before playing game.
2. (a) to take without permission or knowledge; (b) run to base when next batter hasn't hit the ball.
3. (a) a game; (b) touch player with a ball.
4. (a) set something in a different location; (b) cause a player to be out.
5. (a) something to eat on; (b) a marker for home base.
6. (a) run to where you live; (b) run to home plate.
7. (a) know who has the winning points; (b) know the count of balls and strikes.

WALTER EDMONDS: *The Matchlock Gun*

```
Y U O N Z L Z V S G F U Z G F V T M J F
X I H A P F U R S A R T M L F I W B W T T
O J E W P X M U S K E T R F N B R W N Q
Y R R V Y Q L T Q N N J E G W L O D I S S
U X R C I W O F G A C Y K U I N N L U D W
A R D F I O L T U U H J V U N I F O R M S
G F S I B T I J N Y R L Y A T I Q V A A H
R W Z K T S W Y G D T O C A E M S C C W N
V J U Z V S Y Q Z E I M L R Z D J U Y N
S L A F A V U Q T D R A I L J L T R D I L
W W A G C E P I E H P T N L A H J U P H H
B M Z T I U B J Z G O C R S I N R S O G J
K T I Y X W B H N L W H O U A D W G L I
Y L Y O O T A F C T D L O C D K I L R W H
H K I Z R D A A H R E O V J Q P A G K V
Y N S D J N T Q A L R C G J B V D J E Q N
N P J N L L P W B X Q K Y B Y Z J L Q P D
X Z M J W K D Y S M O L O O H G Z H X R W
B R I D G E M A H T F Z S S M J X O L V N
```

July Answer Key

RICHARD EGIELSKI: *Mary's Mirror*

1. happy
2. mirror
3. looked
4. frock
5. hat
6. gloves
7. boots

8. chain
9. last
10. traded
11. broke
12. song
13. poor

MARGERY WILLIAMS: *The Velveteen Rabbit: Or How Toys Become Real*

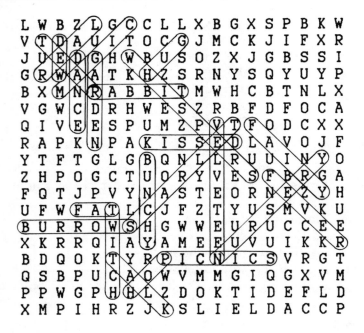

PATRICIA COOMBS: *Dorrie and the Blue Witch*

1. crooked
2. kitchen
3. shrink
4. cloak
5. fist

6. bee
7. bottle
8. piano
9. polite
10. cauldron

July Answer Key

ROBERT QUACKENBUSH: *Dig to Disaster*

1. Harold Scoter
2. A cable broke and it collapsed.
3. The dugout canoe sprang a leak.
4. Harold Scoter
5. A loud blare of a jungle horn
6. A headless demon
7. Tire tracks
8. She sat on a rock.
9. Harold Scoter
10. He wanted the treasure for himself.

JAN BERENSTAIN: *The Berenstain Bears Go to Camp*

1. vacation
2. camp
3. lake
4. logs
5. rules
6. canoe
7. frame
8. cave
9. legend
10. trophy

BEATRIX POTTER: *The Tale of Peter Rabbit*

1. tree
2. garden
3. pie
4. bakery
5. Peter
6. beans; radishes lettuce
7. rake
8. shoes
9. can
10. gate
11. cold
12. tea; bed

JULY AUTHORS BIBLIOGRAPHY

July 2   Jack Gantos

All published by Houghton Mifflin: *Rotten Ralph* (1976); *Worse than Rotten, Ralph* (1982); *Rotten Ralph's Rotten Christmas* (1984); *Rotten Ralph's Trick or Treat* (1986).

July 10   Julian May (also writes as Ian Thorne)

Has rewritten story lines from monster hits of yesteryear, published by Crestwood House, and with original black-and-white photographs: "The Blob," "Frankenstein," "Dracula," "Mad Scientists," and many more; has also written on such nonfiction topics as ancient astronauts and UFOs.

July 11   E. B. White

Great for advanced second and third grade readers who want a challenge: *Stuart Little* (Harper, 1945); *Charlotte's Web* (Harper, 1952).

July 13   Marcia Brown

Stone Soup (Macmillan, 1947)—1948 Caldecott Honor book; translated and illustrated *Cinderella, or the Little Glass Slipper* by Charles Perrault (Scribner's, 1954)—1955 Caldecott Award winner; *Once a Mouse* (Scribner's, 1961)—1962 Caldecott Award winner; illustrated *Shadow* translated by Blaise Cendrars (Scribner's, 1982)—1983 Caldecott Award winner.

July 14   Peggy Parish

Children will learn that Amelia Bedelia takes everything literally! She makes sponge cake out of sponges. When her boss tells her to go fly a kite, she does! *Come Back, Amelia Bedelia* (Harper, 1978); *Play Ball, Amelia Bedelia* (Harper, 1978); *Teach Us, Amelia Bedelia* (Harper, 1978); *Amelia Bedelia and the Suprise Shower* (Harper, 1979); *Clues in the Woods* (Dell, 1980); *Key to the Treasure* (Dell, 1980); *Amelia Bedelia and the Baby* (Greenwillow, 1981); *No More Monsters for Me* (Harper, 1981); *Good Work, Amelia Bedelia* (Avon, 1982); *Amelia Bedelia Helps Out* (Avon, 1982); *Amelia Bedelia* (Harper, 1983); *Thank You, Amelia Bedelia* (Harper, 1983); *Amelia Bedelia Goes Camping* (Avon, 1986); *Merry Christmas, Amelia Bedelia* (Greenwillow, 1986).

July 15   Walter Edmonds

The Matchlock Gun (Dodd, 1941)—1942 Newbery Award winner.

July Authors Bibliography

July 15   Clement C. Moore

The Night Before Christmas has been published in many editions and has been illustrated by many different illustrators including Leonard Weisgard, Cindy Szekeres, Anita Lobel, James Marshall, Michael Hague, Tomie DePaola, and Tasha Tudor.

July 16   Richard Egielski

Illustrated: *Sid & Sol* by Arthur Yorinks (Farrar, 1977); *Louis the Fish* by Arthur Yorinks (Farrar, 1980); *Mary's Mirror* by Jim Aylesworth (Holt, 1982); *It Happened in Pinsk* by Arthur Yorinks (Farrar, 1983); *Hey, Al* by Arthur Yorinks (Farrar, 1986)—1987 Caldecott Award winner.

July 16   Eve Titus

Anatole (McGraw-Hill, 1956—out of print)—1957 Caldecott Honor book; Anatole series published by McGraw-Hill; Basil series published by Archway for grades 2-3.

July 19   Eve Merriam

Birthday Cow (Knopf, 1978); *Good Night to Annie* (Four Winds Press, 1980); *Christmas Box* (Morrow, 1985); *Sky Full of Poems* (Dell, 1986).

July 22   Margery Williams

The Velveteen Rabbit (Little Simon, 1986).

July 23   Patricia Coombs

Dorrie, the cute little witch, series published by Dell (originally by Lothrop); *Dorrie & the Amazing Magic Elixir, Dorrie & the Blue Witch, Dorrie & the Halloween Plot, Dorrie & the Museum Case, Dorrie & the Witch Doctor, Dorrie & the Witches' Camp.*

July 23   Robert Quackenbush

Henry series published by Parents: *Henry Babysits, Henry Goes West, Henry's Awful Mistake*; Piet Potter mysteries published by McGraw-Hill: *Piet Potter Rescue: Book 1, Piet Potter Strikes Again: Book 2, Piet Potter to the Rescue*; Miss Mallard mysteries published by Prentice Hall: *Dig to Disaster, Express Train to Trouble, Gondola to Danger, Rickshaw to Horror.*

July 26   Jan Berenstain

Berenstain Bear series written with Stan Berenstain published by Random House.

July Authors Bibliography

July 27 Scott Corbett

Easy, humorous mysteries for good third grade readers: *The Disappearing Dog Trick* (Scholastic, 1983); *Hangman's Ghost Trick* (Scholastic, 1983); *Hairy Horror Trick* (Scholastic, 1985).

July 28 Natalie Babbitt

Intermediate and advanced author who has something to offer the younger crowd in grades 2-3: *The Something* (Farrar, 1970); *The Devil's Storybook* (Farrar, 1974); *The Devil's Other Storybook* (Farrar, 1987).

July 28 Beatrix Potter

Peter Rabbit classic favorites for grades K-3 published by Warne.

July 31 Muriel Feelings

Mojo Means One (Dial, 1971); *Jambo Means Hello* (Dial, 1981).

 # AUGUST

AUGUST AUTHORS

DATE	NAME	AUTHOR	ILLUSTRATOR	K	1	2	3
2	James Howe	X		X	X	X	X
3	Mary Calhoun	X			X	X	
5	Robert Bright	X	X		X	X	
6	Frank Asch	X	X	X	X		
7	Betsy Byars	X			X	X	
8	Trinka Hakes Noble	X			X	X	X
8	Jan Pienkowski	X	X	X	X		
9	Jose Aruego		X				
11	Don Freeman	X	X		X	X	X
11	Steven Kroll	X			X	X	X
11	Johanna Cole	X			X	X	X
11	Jane Thayer	X			X	X	X
12	Deborah Howe	X					X
14	Robert Crowe	X			X	X	X
14	Alice Provensen	X	X	X	X	X	X
15	Mark Taylor	X			X	X	X
15	Brinton Turkle	X	X		X	X	X
16	Matt Christopher	X					X
17	Ariane Dewey (Aruego)		X		X	X	X
18	Louise Fatio	X			X	X	X
21	Arthur Yorinks	X			X	X	X
26	Bernard Wiseman	X			X	X	X
27	Graham Oakley	X	X		X	X	X
28	Roger Duvoisin	X	X	X	X	X	
28	Ferdinand Monjo	X	X		X	X	
28	Tasha Tudor	X	X	X	X	X	
30	Laurent de Brunhoff	X	X	X	X	X	
30	Virginia Lee Burton	X	X	X	X	X	

JAMES HOWE

"There's a Monster Under My Bed"

Read "There's a Monster Under My Bed." Use the words in the Word Bank to finish these sentences about a little boy who does find something under his bed.

1. Simon heard _____ under his bed.

2. He knew it was a _____.

3. He felt the mattress _____.

4. Two monsters would fight over who could _____ him.

5. Three monsters were sharpening their _____.

6. Four were building a _____ to fry him.

7. Simon would be their midnight _____.

8. His mother left him a _____.

9. He saw two _____ looking at him.

10. It was _____.

11. His brother said he felt _____.

12. Simon was very _____ to sleep with his _____.

```
WORD BANK
Alex      breathing    brother    claws      eat       eyes
fire      flashlight   happy      monster    move      safe      snack
```

Name_____   Date_____

FRANK ASCH

"Moongame" and "Mooncake"

Read "Moongame" and "Mooncake." Find the words from both stories in the word search puzzle below.

```
J W I S H F U D Q C G R O O Q Y V G R A F
H E L P Q O X P D V V Z W F H W G P G A Q A
A R R O W P V N K W G K L G X X J C A C L L
D S N O W H A H D Y O V O X W I L P E O T L
R H U N G R Y I R A G E M A E W T P O T U E
S D V C L O U D J I W T X L W H V T Z J T F
F A G Y W C T E M I N H F N C H H Z T U H B
D L A A A K R Y T R D N W A P J K J Y A E B
W O M S L E E P O O A A S W Y A R T W K W W
J S E E K T E B O W E F T H Z Q I S K Y C
X T I S W Q I I K Y A B G T U P G A K A W
G D S F A V E R K Q S Q U T J B E N E W M
I Y K B D S C D W I S N K U J Q G Q V X X O
C O T Y O Y E Z S S M K P F X P O S K K L O
X Q P O R D E U D G C R Q R I V G T A L N
Q G F G M T M N G C M O E X V W I P E A E
M V H Q T C E Q M U P V D L C O T B E A R
I W Y G O A M V P Z I U C A I T W B Q K N
S N H Q F D B E H O M V I S L L B I T E W
```

WORD BANK					
arrow	bear	bird	bite	bow	cloud
fall	game	help	hide	hungry	lost
moon	rocket	seek	sleep	snow	spoon
tree	walk	wish	cake		

Name_____ Date_____

TRINKA HAKES NOBLE

"The Day Jimmy's Boa Ate the Wash"

Read "The Day Jimmy's Boa Ate the Wash." Use the words in the Word Bank to finish these sentences about a field trip to the farm that was anything but boring.

1. The cow cried because a _____ fell on her.

2. The _____ knocked it over on her.

3. The _____ was yelling at the kids.

4. The kids were yelling at the _____ eating their lunches.

5. The kids threw _____ because they ran out of _____.

6. Jimmy's _____ scared a _____.

7. She laid an egg on Jenny's _____.

8. Jimmy's boa found the _____.

9. It scared the farmer's _____.

10. Jimmy forgot his boa, but loved his new _____.

```
WORD BANK
boa     corn    eggs    farmer    haystack    head
hen     pet     pigs    tractor   wash        wife
```

Name_____   Date_____

DON FREEMAN

"A Rainbow of My Own"

FOR THE TEACHER, LIBRARIAN, MEDIA SPECIALIST

Don Freeman's "A Rainbow of My Own" is a colorful way to say hello to kindergarten children when school starts. Here's how I do it.

1. I introduce myself and read "A Rainbow of My Own.

2. I explain that a rainbow is a symbol of promise—Noah's Ark, a symbol of love, and a symbol of friendship. And I let them know I have a promise, love and friendship for them.

PROMISE: I promise to find each person a good book when they visit me.

LOVE: I love kids. I love my job. and I love good books

FRIENDSHIP: Friends help one another, listen to one another, trust one another, and work together.

3. Then I personally introduce myself to each child and ask their name. We shake hands and begin our friendship on the first visit.

4. Then I give each child a rainbow name tag. They are already colored for them. It usually takes one or two days as I generally have over 120 kindergarten students. I attach them to their shirt or blouse with masking tape. No pins in kindergarten! If you have a preschool group, this activity can also be used with them.

5. If you do this activity with first graders at the beginning of the year, they could very well color their own name tags.

6. And of course—they check out a book by one of our many talented August authors. If you're one of the lucky ones to start school in September, use this activity anyway!

7. Reproduce the rainbow name tag for each child. There is a sheet of them on the next page.

FRIENDSHIP IS A RAINBOW

BETWEEN YOU AND ME!

FRIENDSHIP IS A RAINBOW

BETWEEN YOU AND ME!

FRIENDSHIP IS A RAINBOW

BETWEEN YOU AND ME!

FRIENDSHIP IS A RAINBOW

BETWEEN YOU AND ME!

DON FREEMAN

"A Rainbow of My Own"

STEVEN KROLL

"The Tyrannosaurus Game"

Read "The Tyrannosaurus Game." What a great story. And it's the kind that makes me want to write one too. How about you? I'll start a story just like Jimmy did and you pass it on to a friend, and on and on.

To make your story something very special, write it down so no one forgets what he or she added. Good luck and have fun.

THE GREEN HIPPO

When I got on the bus this morning, I sat next to a green hippo. I couldn't believe it. I wasn't too worried since Thursday was Halloween. I thought it was Sandy. But when Sandy got on the bus, she said, "Who's in the hippo costume?"

I said, "…..

Sandy said, "….

Name_____   **Date**_____

ROBERT CROWE

"Clyde Monster"

Read "Clyde Monster." Aren't you glad people and monsters made a deal a long time ago not to frighten one another? This cute story has a safe, happy ending. But let's change all that! Let's change the ending to one of those below. You pick the ending you like best and give "Clyde Monster" a new ending. Write the new ending on a clean piece of paper.

1. As Clyde is just about to fall asleep, a little boy or girl crawls out from under his bed and says, "Excuse me. Can you show me the way out of this cave?"

2. Clyde wakes up in the middle of the night. He goes to the pond for a drink of water. He sees a little boy or girl in the forest. He runs home quickly. He tells his parents, but they say it was a bad dream. The little person follows Clyde to the cave. Why?

3. Clyde strings a rope with pots and pans on it around his bed. It is his "people trap." What does he really catch? How did it get in there. What happens after that?

Name _____ **Date** _____

ALICE PROVENSEN

"The Glorious Flight Across the Channel
with Louis Bleriot"

Read "The Glorious Flight Across the Channel with Louis Bleriot." Use the words in the Word Bank to finish these sentences about a man who builds and flies airplanes.

1. Louis took a ride in his _____.

2. He saw an _____.

3. He decided to _____ a _____.

4. The wings of the first _____ like a chicken's wings.

5. The second was a _____.

6. A motorboat pulled it over the _____. It crashed.

7. Bleriot V hopped like a _____.

8. Number seven could really _____.

9. He wanted to be first across the English _____.

10. He had to travel _____ miles.

11. He flew in Bleriot _____.

12. He landed in England _____ minutes later.

13. It was a _____ flight for Bleriot!

WORD BANK					
airship	build	Channel	eleven (XI)	flapped	fly
glider	glorious	lake	plane	rabbit	
thirty-seven	car	twenty			

Name_____ Date_____

© 1989 by The Center for Applied Research in Education

BRINTON TURKLE

"Thy Friend, Obadiah"

Read "Thy Friend, Obadiah." Use the words in the Word Bank to finish these sentences about a little boy who has a seagull friend.

1. Obadiah was followed by a _____.

2. At night, he could see it on a _____.

3. Obadiah threw a _____ at it.

4. When Obadiah went to the _____, the bird didn't follow him.

5. Obadiah tried to _____ on a patch of ice.

6. Even the flour got _____.

7. Not one seagull _____ at him.

8. Obadiah was sad about not _____ his seagull.

9. He found it at the _____.

10. It had a _____ line around its _____.

11. Obadiah _____ the line and hook.

12. That night, Obadiah saw his _____ sitting on the chimney once again.

WORD BANK					
beak	chimney	fishing	friend	looked	mill
pebble	removed	seagull	seeing	slide	wet	wharf

Name _____   Date _____

ARTHUR YORINKS

"Hey, Al" and "It Happened in Pinsk"

Read "Hey, Al" and "It Happened in Pinsk." These two stories are very similar. Answer these questions about the stories. The first blank is for "Hey, Al." The second blank is for "It Happened in Pinsk."

1. Who isn't happy in the story?

_____   _____

2. What does he do for a living?

_____   _____

3. What do the characters want?

_____   _____

4. How does each character change?

_____   _____

5. What did they both learn?

_____   _____

Name_____   **Date**_____

ROGER DUVOISIN

"Petunia, I Love You"

Read "Petunia, I Love You." Ooh—that nasty raccoon wanted to eat our dear sweet Petunia. But that was not to be. Each time the raccoon had a plan, something went wrong. The plans are listed below. Write on the lines what happened to spoil raccoon's feast.

1. He planned to jump on her neck when they crossed the tree bridge, but

_____

2. He showed her how to put her head in a hollow of a tree, but

_____

3. He planned to roll a rock on her as she kissed a rock 20 times and made 20 wishes, but

_____

4. He planned to bang her head by jumping hard on a seesaw plank, but

_____

_____

5. Even though raccoon had a bad day, Petunia was sweet enough to let him out of the

_____ .

Name _____   **Date** _____

VIRGINIA LEE BURTON

"The Little House"

Read "The Little House." Use the words in the Word Bank to finish these sentences about a little house that wishes to see the city.

1. A little house was built in the _____.

2. She watched the sun _____ and _____.

3. She watched the stars _____.

4. She wondered what the _____ was like.

5. In the spring, the children played in the _____.

6. In the summer, they _____ in the pool.

7. In the _____, they went back to _____.

8. In the winter, she watched them _____.

9. As time passed, there were more _____ and a _____.

10. Soon the city _____ her.

11. A great, great _____ found the house.

12. They _____ her back to the country

13. They _____ her and _____ her shutters.

WORD BANK

brook	city	country	fall	fixed	granddaughter
houses	moved	painted	rise	road	school
set	skate	surrounded	swam	twinkle	

Name_____ Date_____

  august readers

 time to read

return books on time!

 stop forgetting.

return books on time!

 keep books safe

and dry!

don't cut, color, or crumple

AUGUST ANSWER KEY

JAMES HOWE: *There's a Monster Under My Bed*

1. breathing
2. monster
3. move
4. eat
5. claws
6. fire
7. snack
8. flashlight
9. eyes
10. Alex
11. safe
12. happy; brother

FRANK ASCH: *Moongame* and *Mooncake*

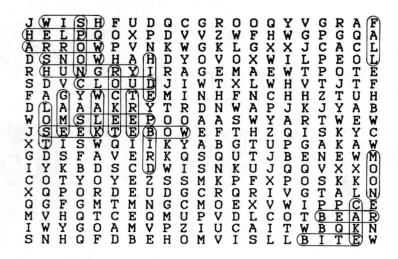

TRINKA HAKES NOBLE: *The Day Jimmy's Boa Ate the Wash*

1. haystack
2. tractor
3. farmer
4. pigs
5. corn; eggs
6. boa; hen
7. head
8. wash
9. wife
10. pet

ALICE PROVENSEN: *The Glorious Flight Across the Channel with Louis Bleriot*

1. car
2. airship
3. build; plane
4. flapped
5. glider
6. lake
7. rabbit
8. fly
9. Channel
10. 20
11. 11 (XI)
12. 37
13. glorious

August Answer Key

BRINTON TURKLE: *Thy Friend, Obadiah*

1. seagull
2. chimney
3. pebble
4. mill
5. slide
6. wet
7. looked
8. seeing
9. wharf
10. fishing; beak
11. removed
12. friend

ARTHUR YORINKS: *Hey, Al* and *It Happened in Pinsk*

1. Al; Irv
2. Janitor; shoe salesman
3. A better life; a better life
4. Al changes into a bird; he loses his head
5. There's no place like home; don't complain; be happy

ROGER DUVOISIN: *Petunia, I Love You*

1. The tree bridge broke.
2. The bees chased him.
3. The rock rolled back on him.
4. He flew into the air instead.
5. cage.

VIRGINIA LEE BURTON: *The Little House*

1. country
2. rise; set
3. twinkle
4. city
5. brook
6. swam
7. fall; school
8. skate
9. houses; road
10. surrounded
11. granddaughter
12. moved
13. fixed; painted

AUGUST AUTHORS BIBLIOGRAPHY

August 2   James Howe

Well-known author for grades 3-6 has new titles for younger readers and storytime: *The Day the Teacher Went Bananas* (Dutton, 1984); *There's a Monster Under My Bed* (Macmillan, 1986); *I Wish I Were a Butterfly* (HBJ, 1987).

August 3   Mary Calhoun

Another intermediate author adds her flair to grades K-3: *Wobble the Witch Cat* (Morrow, 1958); *Hungry Leprechaun* (Morrow, 1962); *The Witch of Hissing Hill* (Morrow, 1964); *Cross-Country Cat* (Morrow, 1979); *The Witch Who Lost Her Shadow* (Harper, 1979); *Audobon Cat* (Morrow, 1981); *Hot-Air Henry* (Morrow, 1981); *Jack and the Whoopie Wind* (Morrow, 1987).

August 5   Robert Bright

Georgie the Little Ghost series published by Doubleday; *My Red Umbrella* (Morrow, 1959).

August 6   Frank Asch

Easy-to-read Bear series for grades 1-2 published by Prentice Hall: *Bear Shadow, Bear's Bargain, Bread & Honey, Mooncake, Moongame, Goodnight Moon, Horsey, Skyfire; Country Pie and City Sandwich* (Greenwillow, 1979); *Turtle Tale* (Dial, 1980).

August 7   Betsy Byars

Author of books for grades K-8, these two are for K-3: *Go and Hush the Baby* (Penguin, 1982); *Golly Sisters Go West* (Harper, 1986).

August 8   Trinka Hakes Noble

The Day Jimmy's Boa Ate the Wash, illustrated by Steven Kellogg (Dial, 1980); *Karin's Christmas Walk* (Dial, 1983); *Hansy's Mermaid* (Dial, 1983); *Jimmy's Boa Bounces Back* (Dial, 1984); *Apple Tree Christmas* (Dial, 1984); *Meanwhile Back at the Ranch* (Dial, 1987).

August 8   Jan Pienkowski

Big, bright, bold illustrations in tiny books published by Simon & Schuster: *ABC, Colors, Home, I'm Cat, I'm Frog, I'm Mouse, I'm Panda, Shapes, Sizes, Time, Weather; Haunted House* (Dutton, 1979); *Robot* (Delacorte, 1981); *Christmas* (Knopf, 1984).

August 9   Jose Aruego

Illustrated many of Robert Kraus' books: *Whose Mouse Are You?* (Macmillan, 1970); *Leo the Late Bloomer* (Crowell, 1971); *Herman the Helper* (Windmill, 1974); *Owliver* (Windmill, 1974); *Milton the Early Riser* (Messner, 1981); illustrated Mirra Ginsburg titles: *How the Sun Was Brought Back to the Sky* (Macmillan, 1975); *Where Does the Sun Go at Night* (Greenwillow, 1980).

August 11   Johanna Cole

A Snake's Body (Morrow, 1981); *The Clown-Arounds* (Parents, 1981); *A Bird's Body* (Morrow, 1982); *A Cat's Body* (Morrow, 1982); *The Clown-Arounds Have a Party* (Parents, 1982); *Bony-Legs* (Macmillan, 1983); *Get Well, Clown-Arounds* (Parents, 1983); *The Clown-Arounds Go on Vacation* (Parents, 1984) *Monster Manners* (Scholastic, 1985); *A Dog's Body* (Morrow, 1986); *Monster Movie* (Scholastic, 1987).

August 11   Don Freeman

Fly High, Fly Low (Viking, 1957)—1958 Caldecott Honor book; *Tilly Witch* (Viking, 1969); *Will's Quill* (Viking, 1975); *Corduroy* (Penguin, 1976); *Dandelion* (Penguin, 1977); *A Pocket for Corduroy* (Viking, 1978); *A Rainbow of My Own* (Penguin, 1978); *Space Witch* (Penguin, 1979).

August 11   Steven Kroll

The Tyrannosaurus Game (Holiday, 1976); *Santa's Crash Bang Christmas* (Holiday, 1977); *Amanda and the Giggling Ghost* (Holiday, 1980); *Space Cats* (Avon, 1981); *Big Bunny & the Easter Eggs* (Scholastic, 1983); *Loose Tooth* (Holiday, 1984); *The Biggest Pumpkin Ever* (Holiday, 1984); *Mrs. Claus's Crazy Christmas* (Holiday, 1985); *Happy Mother's Day* (Holiday, 1985); *Big Bunny & the Magic Show* (Holiday, 1986).

August 11   Jane Thayer

The Puppy Who Wanted a Boy (Morrow, 1958); *Quiet on Account of Dinosaur* (Morrow, 1964); *Gus Was a Real Dumb Ghost* (Morrow, 1982).

August 12   Deborah Howe

Coauthored with James Howe: *Bunnicula: A Rabbit Tale of Mystery* (Macmillan, 1979); *Teddy Bear's Scrapbook* (Macmillan, 1987).

August 14   Robert Crowe

Clyde Monster, illustrated by Kay Chorao (Dutton, 1976); *Tyler Toad and the Thunder*, illustrated by Kay Chorao (Dutton, 1980).

August 14   Alice Provensen

See "July 10, Martin Provensen" for listing.

August Authors Bibliography

August 15   Mark Taylor

Henry the Explorer (Macmillan, 1976); *Mr. Pepper Stories* (Macmillan, 1984); *Case of the Purloined Compass* (Macmillan, 1985).

August 15   Brinton Turkle

Thy Friend, Obadiah (Viking, 1969)—1970 Caldecott Honor book; *The Adventures of Obadiah* (Viking, 1972); *Deep in the Forest* (Dutton, 1976)—a wordless picture book; *Rachel and Obadiah* (Dutton, 1978); *Do Not Open* (Dutton 1981).

August 16   Matt Christopher

Easy reading sports books for third graders, published by Little, Brown: *The Great Quarterback Switch* (1984); *Touchdown for Tommy* (1985); *The Fox Steals Home* (1985); *The Kid Who Only Hit Homers* (1986); *The Year Mom Won the Pennant* (1986); *Ice Magic* (1987).

August 17   Ariane Aruego (also writes as Ariane Dewey)

Illustrated with Jose Aruego: *Chick and the Duckling* (Macmillan, 1972); *Gregory the Terrible Eater* (Macmillan, 1980); *Lizard's Song* (Greenwillow, 1981); *Dance Away* (Greenwillow, 1982); *Alligator Arrived with Apples* (Macmillan, 1987); *Come Out and Play, Little Mouse* (Greenwillow, 1987).

August 18   Louise Fatio

Her husband, Roger Duvoisin, illustrated her books: *Happy Lion* (McGrow, 1964; Scholastic's Blue Ribbon, 1986); *Happy Lion and the Bear* (McGraw, 1964); *Happy Lioness* (McGraw, 1980).

August 21   Arthur Yorinks

See "July 16, Richard Egielski" for listing.

August 26   Bernard Wiseman

Morris the Moose and Boris the Bear series: *Morris Goes to School* (Harper, 1970); *Morris and Boris* (Dodd, 1974); *Halloween with Morris and Boris* (Dodd, 1975); *Morris Tells Boris Mother Moose Stories and Rhymes* (Dodd, 1979).

August 27   Graham Oakley

Church Mice series published by Macmillan: *The Church Mouse, Diary of a Church Mouse, The Church Mice Adrift, The Church Mice and the Moon, The Church Mice at Bay, The Church Mice at Christmas, The Church Mice in Action, Church Cat*; a most ingenious book is *Graham Oakley's Magical Changes* (Macmillan, 1980)—pages are split to make different pictures.

August 28   Roger Duvoisin

Petunia the Goose series published by Knopf: *Petunia, Petunia Beware, Petunia—I Love You, Petunia's Christmas*; Veronica books published by Knopf: *Veronica, Veronica and the Birthday Present, Veronica's Smile*.

August Authors Bibliography

August 28 Ferdinand Monjo

Indian Summer (Harper, 1968); *The Drinking Gourd* (Harper, 1969); *The One Bad Thing About Father* (Harper, 1970); *The Secret of the Sachem's Tree* (Dell, 1970).

August 28 Tasha Tudor

One of the world's greatest illustrators for children and lovers of art in children's books: *Doll's Christmas* (McKay, 1950); *A Is for Anabelle* (Macmillan, 1954); *Tasha Tudor Book of Fairy Tales* (Putnam, 1961); *A Tale for Easter* (McKay, 1973); *Book of Christmas* (Putnam, 1979); more titles are coming out in revised printings, so check the library.

August 30 Laurent de Brunhoff

He continues the series created by his father, Jean de Brunhoff: *Babar Loses His Crown* (Random, 1967); *Babar Learns to Cook* (Random, 1979); *Babar and the Ghost* (Random, 1981); *Babar Visits Another Planet* (Random, 1983); and more.

August 30 Virginia Lee Burton

Mike Mulligan and His Steam Shovel (Houghton Mifflin, 1939); *The Little House* (Houghton Mifflin, 1942)—1943 Caldecott Award winner; *Katy and the Big Snow* (Houghton Mifflin, 1943); *Life Story* (Houghton Mifflin, 1962).